Pro-Life
v.
Pro-Death:
Abortions and the
Supreme Court

Catherine McGrew Jaime

Books by Catherine Jaime include:

- *A Brief Financial History of the United States*
- *A Brief Look at Machiavelli and the Prince*
- *A Celebration of Black History*
- *A Conservative Primer on Government and Economics*
- *A Trial of a Trial* (a Mock Trial Story)
- *Failure in Philadelphia?* (Historical Fiction)
- *Important Constitutional Documents*
- *Notes from Frederick Bastiat's Essays on Political Economy*
- *Simply Put: A Study in Economics* (Student Book and Teacher Key available)
- *The American Revolution and the Declaration of Independence: Founding Era Plays*
- *The Philadelphia Convention: A Play for Many Readers*
- *The Philadelphia Convention: In Their Own Words*
- *There Ought to Be a Law (Or Should There?)*
- *The Rocky Road to Civil Rights in the United States*
- *Understanding Presidential Elections*
- *Understanding the Electoral College*
- *Understanding the U.S. Constitution*
- *U.S. Constitution Topical Study*

Creative Learning Connection
8006 Old Madison Pike, Ste 11-A
Madison, AL 35758
www.CreativeLearningConnection.com

Dedication

This book is dedicated to two of my students, Chloie O. and Sonia J. With their desire to take anti-abortion bills to Youth Legislature, they encouraged me to look into this important topic again.

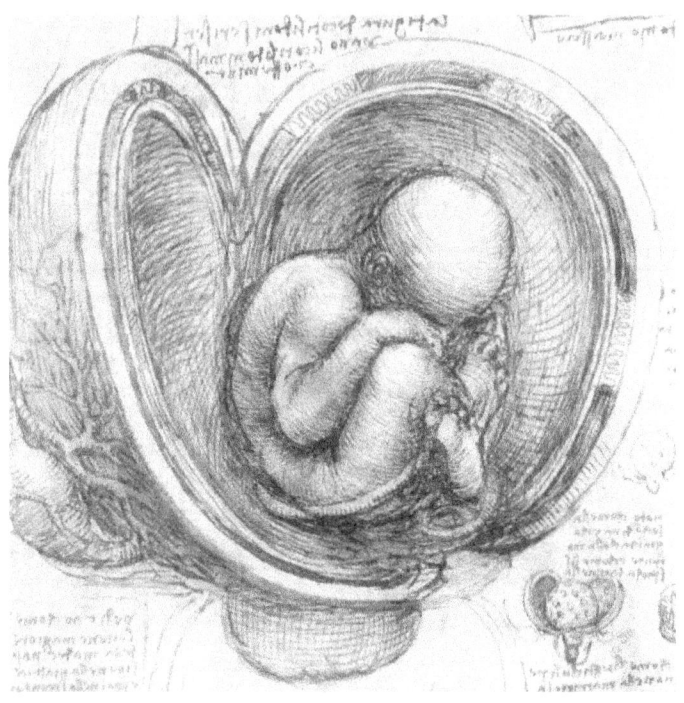

This wonderful sketch of an unborn baby was drawn by Leonardo da Vinci almost exactly 500 years ago. Every time I look at it, I have no doubt that he understood this was indeed a baby!

Table of Contents

Quotes

From Roe v. Wade

"The Constitution does not explicitly mention any right of privacy. In a line of decisions, however, going back perhaps as far as 1891, the Court has recognized that a right of personal privacy, or a guarantee of certain areas or zones of privacy, does exist under the Constitution."

From Blackmun's Majority Opinion

"The fact that a majority of the States reflecting, after all, the majority sentiment in those States, have had restrictions on abortions for at least a century is a strong indication, it seems to me, that the asserted right to an abortion is not 'so rooted in the traditions and conscience of our people as to be ranked as fundamental.'"

From Rehnquist's Dissenting Opinion

From Doe v. Bolton

"Roe v. Wade sets forth our conclusion that a pregnant woman does not have an absolute constitutional right to an abortion on her demand… Further, a physician or any other employee has the right to refrain, for moral or religious reasons, from participating in the abortion procedure."

From Blackmun's Majority Opinion

"The common claim before us is that, for any one of such reasons, or for no reason at all, and without asserting or claiming any threat to life or health, any woman is entitled to an abortion at her request if she is able to find a medical advisor willing to undertake the procedure."
From Justice White's Dissent

From Planned Parenthood v. Casey

"Viability marks the earliest point at which the State's interest in fetal life is constitutionally adequate to justify a legislative ban on nontherapeutic abortions. The soundness or unsoundess of that constitutional judgment in no sense turns on when viability occurs."
From the Majority Opinion

"The correct analysis is that set forth by the plurality opinion in Webster: a woman's interest in having an abortion is a form of liberty protected by the Due Process Clause, but States may regulate abortion procedures in ways rationally related to a legitimate state interest."
From Rehnquist's Minority Opinion

"That is, quite simply, the issue in this case: not whether the power of a woman to abort her unborn child is a "liberty" in the absolute sense; or even whether it is a liberty of great importance to many women. Of course it is both. The issue is whether it is a liberty protected by the Constitution of the United States. I am sure it is not."
From Scalia's Minority Opinion

Introduction

As an adult, I have been well aware of the growing number of abortions in this country – and the impact *Roe v. Wade* had on changing (or halting) the abortion laws across the country. (In fact, I was in high school when the Supreme Court made its infamous decision in *Roe v. Wade.*) But it wasn't until recently, when I really started looking at the actual Supreme Court opinions – both the majority and minority – that I realized exactly what *Roe v. Wade* did and didn't do. And it wasn't until I started helping my students that I realized there were other important Supreme Court cases dealing with abortions.

Two important disclaimers before we get going – I am **not** a lawyer and I **am** a conservative. There are plenty of technical books out there by lawyers dealing with topics such as this, but very few written by non-lawyers for non-lawyers. This is my attempt to help fill that void. And of course, my conservative leanings directly impact what I have chosen to include and not include from these major Supreme Court opinions (though I have not taken things out of context, nor left out parts just because I disagreed with them).

I have chosen to include major excerpts from three of the primary Supreme Court cases dealing with abortion: *Roe v. Wade, Doe v. Bolton,* and *Planned Parenthood v. Casey.* There have been numerous others

3

– and many of those are quoted within these opinions. I have put various parts of both majority and minority opinions in bold – those are portions I found particularly encouraging in some cases, and particularly disconcerting in others. If you want to start small – you may want to start with the Quotes and/or the Abstracts. If you want to get your feet wet without jumping right in to dozens of pages of Opinions – you may want to start with the aforementioned bolded sections.

Several amendments to the U.S. Constitution are mentioned repeatedly in these cases – the First, Fourth, Fifth, Ninth, and Fourteenth. Those are included at the back of the book for easy reference.

I have tried to take out most of the "legalese" – but sometimes they were a critical part of the opinion, so I left them in – hopefully those will be clear from their context. There are frequent references to the **appellants** – those are the ones who claimed the law in question was unconstitutional – they are the ones listed first in a case title, so for instance Roe, Doe, and Planned Parenthood are the appellants in the above cases. The **appellees** are those who are arguing to keep the law in place – generally representing some portion of the government – so in the above cases Wade, Bolton, and Casey are the appellees. There is also an occasional mention of **amici** – those are "friends of the court" – not directly involved, but offering arguments for one side or the other – generally because they have a stake in the outcome.

I have not included the footnotes and endnotes from the opinions, and I have taken the liberty of not only abridging the opinions, but also rearranging some of the sections (preferring to have things like the definition of abortion and the history of abortions towards the beginning of the book, rather than in the midst of the opinions where they originally appeared). I have included a small number of footnotes of my own, primarily with the names of specific cases that the Supreme Court referred to. The entire, unedited opinions for all these Supreme Court cases are available in various places on-line.

One of my primary goals here is to help other "pro-lifers" understand what we actually lost with these Supreme Court cases and to consider what we still could be doing to help bring abortions back down from their current staggering numbers.

While I found much of what I read in these opinions to be very discouraging, I did find places of hope – and not just among the dissenting opinions. Majority opinions talked of "viability" often, insisted they were not authorizing abortions on demand, and even accepted other limitations on abortion. Somehow it seems that all of that has been missed in this continued discussion. When I finished reading these opinions, for the first time since *Roe v. Wade* first impacted our abortion laws, I feel hope that we can accomplish something positive in this area!

Following this introduction you will find one to two page Abstracts for each of those cases – highlighting some of the best/worst that I found in each of them.

"A person is a person no matter how small."

Dr. Seuss, *Horton Hears a Who*

Abstract of Roe v. Wade

In 1973, in a 7-2 decision, the Supreme Court of the United States declared a Texas law that banned most abortions to be unconstitutional. The District Court had struck down the law as a 9th Amendment violation, but the Supreme Court found that it violated the 14th Amendment.

The following excerpts are from the Majority Opinion, authored by Justice Blackmun:

"We, therefore, conclude that the right of personal privacy includes the abortion decision, but that this right is not unqualified, and must be considered against important state interests in regulation."

"With respect to the State's important and legitimate interest in potential life, the 'compelling' point is at viability. This is so because the fetus then presumably has the capability of meaningful life outside the mother's womb. State regulation protective of fetal life after viability thus has both logical and biological justifications."

Justice Rehnquist and Justice White both dissented. Justice Rehnquist wrote the following in his opinion:

"I have difficulty in concluding, as the Court does, that the right of "privacy" is involved in this case...Nor is the "privacy" that the Court finds here even a distant relative of the freedom from searches and seizures protected by the Fourth Amendment to the Constitution, which the Court has referred to as embodying a right to privacy."

Justice White's dissent included these powerful words:

"At the heart of the controversy in these cases are those recurring pregnancies that pose no danger whatsoever to the life or health of the mother but are, nevertheless, unwanted for any one or more of a variety of reasons — convenience, family planning, economics, dislike of children, the embarrassment of illegitimacy, etc."

"I find nothing in the language or history of the Constitution to support the Court's judgment. The Court simply fashions and announces a new constitutional right for pregnant mothers and, with scarcely any reason or authority for its action, invests that right with sufficient substance to override most existing state abortion statutes. The upshot is that the people and the legislatures of the 50 States are constitutionally dissentitled to weigh the relative importance of the continued existence and development of the fetus, on the one hand, against a spectrum of possible impacts on the mother, on the other hand."

Abstract of Doe v. Bolton

Also in 1973, in another 7-2 decision, the Supreme Court of the United States, declared several portions of Georgia's abortion law to be unconstitutional (while at the same time permitting some).

The following excerpts are from Justice Blackmun's Majority Opinion:

"We agree with the District Court, that the medical judgment may be exercised in the light of all factors—physical, emotional, psychological, familial, and the woman's age—relevant to the wellbeing of the patient. All these factors may relate to health. This allows the attending physician the room he needs to make his best medical judgment. And it is room that operates for the benefit, not the disadvantage, of the pregnant woman."

The following excerpts are from the Concurring Opinion, authored by Justice Douglas:

"Second is freedom of choice in the basic decisions of one's life respecting marriage, divorce, procreation, contraception, and the education and upbringing of children. These rights, unlike those protected by the First Amendment, are subject to some control by the police power. Thus, the Fourth Amendment speaks only of "unreasonable searches and seizures" and of "probable cause." These rights are "fundamental," and we have held that in order to support legislative action the statute must be narrowly and precisely drawn and that a "compelling state interest" must be shown in support of the limitation."

"While childbirth endangers the lives of some women, voluntary abortion at any time and place regardless of medical standards would impinge on a rightful concern of society. The woman's health is part of that concern; as is the life of the fetus after quickening. These concerns justify the State in treating the procedure as a medical one…The right to seek advice on one's health and the right to place reliance on the physician of one's choice are basic to Fourteenth Amendment values."

Justice White's Dissent included these words:

"The Court apparently values the convenience of the pregnant mother more than the continued existence and development of the life or potential life that she carries…In a sensitive area such as this, involving as it does issues over which reasonable men may easily and heatedly differ, I cannot accept the Court's exercise of its clear power of choice by interposing a constitutional barrier to state efforts to protect human life and by investing mothers and doctors with the constitutionally protected right to exterminate it. This issue, for the most part, should be left with the people and to the political processes the people have devised to govern their affairs."

Abstract of Planned Parenthood v. Casey

Nineteen years later, a very divided Court ruled on the constitutionality of a Pennsylvania abortion law, again keeping a small portion, but throwing out most of it:

The Majority Opinion spoke much of the Court's need to retain legitimacy, and pushed hard to explain how dangerous it would be for them to overturn *Roe v. Wade*:

"The Court's power lies, rather, in its legitimacy, a product of substance and perception that shows itself in the people's acceptance of the Judiciary as fit to determine what the Nation's law means, and to declare what it demands."

"The underlying substance of this legitimacy is of course the warrant for the Court's decisions in the Constitution and the lesser sources of legal principle on which the Court draws. That substance is expressed in the Court's opinions, and our contemporary understanding is such that a decision without principled justification would be no judicial act at all."

"Despite the variety of reasons that may inform and justify a decision to overrule, we cannot forget that such a decision is usually perceived (and perceived correctly) as, at the least, a statement that a prior decision was wrong. There is a limit to the amount of error that can plausibly be imputed to prior Courts."

"A decision to overrule Roe's essential holding under the existing circumstances would address error, if error there was, at the cost of both profound and unnecessary damage to the Court's legitimacy, and to the Nation's commitment to the rule of law. It is therefore imperative to adhere to the essence of Roe's original decision, and we do so today."

The divided majority even came up with this to say as to why they couldn't possibly overturn Roe:

"The Roe rule's limitation on state power could not be repudiated without serious inequity to people who, for two decades of economic and social developments, have organized intimate relationships and made choices that define their views of themselves and their places in society, in reliance on the availability of abortion in the event that contraception should fail. The ability of women to participate equally in the economic and social life of the Nation has been facilitated by their ability to control their reproductive lives. The Constitution serves human values, and while the effect of reliance on Roe cannot be exactly measured, neither can the certain costs of overruling Roe for people who have ordered their thinking and living around that case be dismissed."

Chief Justice Rehnquist had this to say about their reasoning in his Minority Opinion:

"And the historical traditions of the American people - as evidenced by the English common law and by the American abortion statutes in existence both at the time of the Fourteenth Amendment's adoption and Roe's issuance - do not support the view that the right to terminate one's pregnancy is 'fundamental.' Thus, enactments abridging that right need not be subjected to strict scrutiny."

"For the same reason, this Court's previous holding invalidating a State's 24-hour mandatory waiting period should not be followed. The waiting period helps ensure that a woman's decision to abort is a well-considered one, and rationally furthers the State's legitimate interest in maternal health and in unborn life. It may delay, but does not prohibit, abortions; and both it and the informed consent provisions do not apply in medical emergencies."

But Scalia's Opinion held the strongest words on the topic:

"The States may, if they wish, permit abortion on demand, but the Constitution does not require them to do so. The permissibility of abortion, and the limitations upon it, are to be resolved like most important questions in our democracy: by citizens trying to persuade one another and then voting. As the Court acknowledges, "where reasonable people disagree, the government can adopt one position or the other.""

"A State's choice between two positions on which reasonable people can disagree is constitutional even when (as is often the case) it intrudes upon a "liberty" in the absolute sense."

"That is, quite simply, the issue in this case: not whether the power of a woman to abort her unborn child is a "liberty" in the absolute sense; or even whether it is a liberty of great importance to many women. Of course it is both. The issue is whether it is a liberty protected by the Constitution of the United States. I am sure it is not."

"The whole argument of abortion opponents is that what the Court calls the fetus and what others call the unborn child is a human life. Thus, whatever answer Roe came up with after conducting its "balancing" is bound to be wrong, unless it is correct that the human fetus is in some critical sense merely potentially human. There is, of course, no way to determine that as a legal matter; it is, in fact, a value judgment. Some societies have considered newborn children not yet human, or the incompetent elderly no longer so."

Roe v. Wade

Jane Roe, et al.

v.

Henry Wade, District Attorney of Dallas County

Argued December 13, 1971
Reargued October 11, 1972
Decided January 22, 1973

Primary Case Opinions

Majority: Blackmun, joined by Burger, Douglas, Brennan, Steward, Marshall, Powell

Dissent: White, joined by Rehnquist

Definition of Abortion
(From the Texas Law, Quoted in *Roe v. Wade*)

If any person shall designedly administer to a pregnant woman or knowingly procure to be administered without her consent any drug or medicine, or shall use towards her any violence or means whatever externally or internally applied, and thereby procure an abortion, he shall be confined in the penitentiary not less than two nor more than five years; if it be done without her consent, the punishment shall be doubled. By 'abortion' is meant that the life of the fetus or embryo shall be destroyed in the woman's womb or that a premature birth thereof be caused.

Additional Notes by Justice Blackmun In his Majority Opinion

We forthwith acknowledge our awareness of the sensitive and emotional nature of the abortion controversy, of the vigorous opposing views, even among physicians, and of the deep and seemingly absolute convictions that the subject inspires. One's philosophy, one's experiences, one's exposure to the raw edges of human existence, one's religious training, one's attitudes toward life and family and their values, and the moral standards one establishes and seeks to observe, are all likely to influence and to color one's thinking and conclusions about abortion.

In addition, population growth, pollution, poverty, and racial overtones tend to complicate and not to simplify the problem...

[The Constitution] is made for people of fundamentally differing views, and the accident of our finding certain opinions natural and familiar or novel and even shocking ought not to conclude our judgment upon the question whether statutes embodying them conflict with the Constitution of the United States.

The History of Abortion
(Also from Justice Blackmun's Majority Opinion in *Roe v. Wade*)

Before addressing this claim, we feel it desirable briefly to survey, in several aspects, the history of abortion, for such insight as that history may afford us, and then to examine the state purposes and interests behind the criminal abortion laws…

1. *Ancient attitudes*…We are told that, at the time of the Persian Empire, abortifacients were known, and that criminal abortions were severely punished. We are also told, however, that abortion was practiced in Greek times as well as in the Roman Era, and that "it was resorted to without scruple." The Ephesian, Soranos, often described as the greatest of the ancient gynecologists, appears to have been generally opposed to Rome's prevailing free-abortion practices. He found it necessary to think first of the life of the mother, and he resorted to abortion when, upon this standard, he felt the procedure advisable. Greek and Roman law afforded little protection to the unborn. If abortion was prosecuted in some places, it seems to have been based on a concept of a violation of the father's right to his offspring…

2. *The Hippocratic Oath.* What then of the famous Oath that has stood so long as the ethical guide of the medical profession…The Oath varies somewhat according to the particular translation, but in any translation the content is clear:

> *I will neither give a deadly drug to anybody if asked for it, nor will I make a suggestion to this effect. Similarly, I will not give to a woman an abortive remedy.*

Although the Oath is not mentioned in any of the principal briefs in this case or in *Doe v. Bolton*, it represents the apex of the development of strict ethical concepts in medicine, and its influence endures to this day…[But], the Oath was not uncontested even in Hippocrates' day; only the Pythagorean school of philosophers frowned upon the related act of suicide. Most Greek thinkers, on the other hand, commended abortion, at least prior to viability. For the Pythagoreans, however, it was a matter of dogma. For them, the embryo was animate from the moment of conception, and abortion meant destruction of a living being. The abortion clause of the Oath, therefore, "echoes Pythagorean doctrines"…

But with the end of antiquity, a decided change took place. Resistance against suicide and against abortion became common. The Oath came to be popular. The emerging teachings of Christianity were in agreement with the Pythagorean ethic. The Oath "became the nucleus of all medical ethics," and "was applauded as the embodiment of truth." ...

3. *The common law.* It is undisputed that, at common law, abortion performed before "quickening" — the first recognizable movement of the fetus in utero, appearing usually from the 16th to the 18th week of pregnancy — was not an indictable offense. The absence of a common law crime for pre-quickening abortion appears to have developed from a confluence of earlier philosophical, theological, and civil and canon law concepts of when life begins. These disciplines variously approached the question in terms of the point at which the embryo or fetus became "formed" or recognizably human, or in terms of when a "person" came into being, that is, infused with a "soul" or "animated." A loose consensus evolved in early English law that these events occurred at some point between conception and live birth...

There was agreement, however, that, prior to this point, the fetus was to be regarded as part of the mother, and its destruction, therefore, was not homicide...The significance of quickening was echoed by later common law scholars, and found its way into the received common law in this country.

4. *The English statutory law.* England's first criminal abortion statute, Lord Ellenborough's Act,

came in 1803. It made abortion of a quick fetus, a capital crime, but, it provided lesser penalties for the felony of abortion before quickening, and thus preserved the "quickening" distinction…In 1929, the Infant Life (Preservation) Act, came into being. Its emphasis was upon the destruction of "the life of a child capable of being born alive." It made a willful act performed with the necessary intent a felony. It contained a proviso that one was not to be found guilty of the offense unless it is proved that the act which caused the death of the child was not done in good faith for the purpose only of preserving the life of the mother…

Recently, Parliament enacted a new abortion law. This is the Abortion Act of 1967. The Act permits a licensed physician to perform an abortion where two other licensed physicians agree (a) that the continuance of the pregnancy would involve risk to the life of the pregnant woman, or of injury to the physical or mental health of the pregnant woman or any existing children of her family, greater than if the pregnancy were terminated, or (b) that there is a substantial risk that, if the child were born it would suffer from such physical or mental abnormalities as to be seriously handicapped…

5. *The American law.* In this country, the law in effect in all but a few States until mid-19th century was the preexisting English common law. Connecticut, the first State to enact abortion

legislation, adopted in 1821 that part of Lord Ellenborough's Act that related to a woman "quick with child." The death penalty was not imposed. Abortion before quickening was made a crime in that State only in 1860. In 1828, New York enacted legislation that, in two respects, was to serve as a model for early anti-abortion statutes. First, while barring destruction of an unquickened fetus as well as a quick fetus, it made the former only a misdemeanor, but the latter second-degree manslaughter. Second, it incorporated a concept of therapeutic abortion by providing that an abortion was excused if it shall have been necessary to preserve the life of such mother, or shall have been advised by two physicians to be necessary for such purpose.

By 1840, when Texas had received the common law, only eight American States had statutes dealing with abortion. It was not until after the War Between the States that legislation began generally to replace the common law. Most of these initial statutes dealt severely with abortion after quickening, but were lenient with it before quickening…Gradually, in the middle and late 19th century, the quickening distinction disappeared from the statutory law of most States and the degree of the offense and the penalties were increased. By the end of the 1950's, a large majority of the jurisdictions banned abortion, however and whenever performed, unless done to save or preserve the life of the mother. The exceptions, Alabama and the District of Columbia, permitted abortion to preserve the mother's health...In the past several years, however, a trend toward liberalization of abortion statutes has resulted in adoption, by about one-third of the States, of less stringent laws...

6. *The position of the American Medical Association.* The anti-abortion mood prevalent in this country in the late 19th century was shared by the medical profession. Indeed, the attitude of the profession may have played a significant role in the enactment of stringent criminal abortion legislation during that period.

An AMA Committee on Criminal Abortion was appointed in May, 1857. It presented its report to the Twelfth Annual Meeting. That report observed that the Committee had been appointed to investigate criminal abortion "with a view to its general suppression." It deplored abortion and its frequency and it listed three causes of "this general demoralization":

The first of these causes is a widespread popular ignorance of the true character of the crime — a belief, even among mothers themselves, that the fetus is not alive till after the period of quickening.

The second of the agents alluded to is the fact that the profession themselves are frequently supposed careless of fetal life...

The third reason of the frightful extent of this crime is found in the grave defects of our laws, both common and statute, as regards the independent and actual existence of the child before birth, as a living being…With strange inconsistency, the law fully acknowledges the fetus in utero and its inherent rights, for civil purposes; while personally and as criminally affected, it fails to recognize it, and to its life as yet denies all protection.

The Committee then offered, and the Association adopted, resolutions protesting "against such unwarrantable destruction of human life," calling upon state legislatures to revise their abortion laws, and requesting the cooperation of state medical societies "in pressing the subject."

In 1871, a long and vivid report was submitted by the Committee on Criminal Abortion. It ended with the observation: we had to deal with human life. In a matter of less importance, we could entertain no compromise. An honest judge on the bench would call things by their proper names. We could do no less.

It proffered resolutions, adopted by the Association, recommending, among other things, that it be unlawful and unprofessional for any physician to induce abortion or premature labor without the concurrent opinion of at least one respectable consulting physician, and then always with a view to the safety of the child — if that be possible…

Except for periodic condemnation of the criminal abortionist, no further formal AMA action took place until 1967. In that year, the Committee on Human Reproduction urged the adoption of a stated policy of opposition to induced abortion except when there is "documented medical evidence" of a threat to the health or life of the mother, or that the child "may be born with incapacitating physical deformity or mental deficiency," or that a pregnancy "resulting from legally established statutory or forcible rape or incest may constitute a threat to the mental or physical health of the patient," two other physicians "chosen because of their recognized professional competence have examined the patient and have concurred in writing," and the procedure "is performed in a hospital accredited by the Joint Commission on Accreditation of Hospitals." ...This recommendation was adopted by the House of Delegates.

...On June 25, 1970, the House of Delegates adopted preambles and most of the resolutions proposed by the reference committee. The preambles emphasized "the best interests of the patient," "sound clinical judgment," and "informed patient consent," in contrast to "mere acquiescence to the patient's demand." The resolutions asserted that abortion is a medical procedure that should be performed by a licensed physician in an accredited hospital only after consultation with two other physicians and in conformity with state law, **and that**

no party to the procedure should be required to violate personally held moral principles.

7. *The position of the American Public Health Association.* In October, 1970, the Executive Board of the APHA adopted Standards for Abortion Services...

a. Rapid and simple abortion referral must be readily available through state and local public health departments, medical societies, or other nonprofit organizations.

b. An important function of counseling should be to simplify and expedite the provision of abortion services; it should not delay the obtaining of these services.

c. Psychiatric consultation should not be mandatory...

d. A wide range of individuals from appropriately trained, sympathetic volunteers to highly skilled physicians may qualify as abortion counselors.

e. Contraception and/or sterilization should be discussed with each abortion patient.

Recommended Standards for Abortion Services (1971). Among factors pertinent to life and health risks associated with abortion were three that "are recognized as important":

a. the skill of the physician,

b. the environment in which the abortion is performed, and above all

c. the duration of pregnancy...

It was said that "a well equipped hospital" offers more protection to cope with unforeseen difficulties than an office or clinic without such resources...The factor of gestational age is of overriding importance.

Thus, it was recommended that abortions in the second trimester and early abortions in the presence of existing medical complications be performed in hospitals as inpatient procedures...An abortion in an extramural facility, however, is an acceptable alternative "provided arrangements exist in advance to admit patients promptly if unforeseen complications develop." ...

8. *The position of the American Bar Association.* At its meeting in February, 1972, the ABA House of Delegates approved...the Uniform Abortion Act that had been drafted and approved the preceding August by the Conference of Commissioners on Uniform State Laws...

Abortion in Texas
and the Majority Opinion
(More from Justice Blackmun's Opinion
in *Roe v. Wade*)

Three reasons have been advanced to explain historically the enactment of criminal abortion laws in the 19th century and to justify their continued existence. It has been argued occasionally that these laws were the product of a Victorian social concern to discourage illicit sexual conduct. Texas, however, does not advance this justification in the present case, and it appears that no court or commentator has taken the argument seriously. The appellants...contend, moreover, that this is not a proper state purpose, at all and suggest that, if it were, the Texas statutes are overbroad in protecting it, since the law fails to distinguish between married and unwed mothers.

A second reason is concerned with abortion as a medical procedure. When most criminal abortion laws were first enacted, the procedure was a hazardous one for the woman. This was particularly true prior to the development of antisepsis. Antiseptic techniques, of course, were based on discoveries by Lister, Pasteur, and others first announced in 1867, but were not generally accepted and employed until about the turn of the century. Abortion mortality was high. Even after 1900, and perhaps until as late as the development of antibiotics in the 1940's, standard modern techniques…were not nearly so safe as they are today. Thus, it has been argued that a State's real concern in enacting a criminal abortion law was to protect the pregnant woman, that is, to restrain her from submitting to a procedure that placed her life in serious jeopardy…

The Texas statutes under attack here are typical of those that have been in effect in many States for approximately a century…[These] statutes that concern us…make it a crime to "procure an abortion" …except with respect to "an abortion procured or attempted by medical advice for the purpose of saving the life of the mother." Similar statutes are in existence in a majority of the States.

Texas first enacted a criminal abortion statute in 1854. This was soon modified into language that has remained substantially unchanged to the present time. The final article in each of these compilations provided the same exception…for an abortion by "medical advice for the purpose of saving the life of the mother."

Jane Roe, a single woman who was residing in Dallas County, Texas, instituted this federal action in March 1970 against the District Attorney of the county. She sought a declaratory judgment that the Texas criminal abortion statutes were unconstitutional on their face…

Roe alleged that she was unmarried and pregnant; that she wished to terminate her pregnancy by an abortion "performed by a competent, licensed physician, under safe, clinical conditions"; that she was unable to get a "legal" abortion in Texas because her life did not appear to be threatened by the continuation of her pregnancy; and that she could not afford to travel to another jurisdiction in order to secure a legal abortion under safe conditions. She claimed that the Texas statutes were unconstitutionally vague and that they abridged her right of personal privacy, protected by the First, Fourth, Fifth, Ninth, and Fourteenth Amendments.

[T]he District Court held that the fundamental right of single women and married persons to choose whether to have children is protected by the Ninth Amendment, through the Fourteenth Amendment, and that the Texas criminal abortion statutes were void on their face because they were both unconstitutionally vague and constituted an overbroad infringement of the plaintiffs' Ninth Amendment rights.

…The principal thrust of appellant's attack on the Texas statutes is that they improperly invade a right, said to be possessed by the pregnant woman, to choose to terminate her pregnancy. Appellant would discover this right in the concept of personal "liberty" embodied in the Fourteenth Amendment's Due Process Clause; or in personal, marital, familial, and sexual privacy said to be protected by the Bill of Rights…or among those rights reserved to the people by the Ninth Amendment.[1]

…Appellants…refer to medical data indicating that abortion in early pregnancy, that is, prior to the end of the first trimester, although not without its risk, is now relatively safe. Mortality rates for women undergoing early abortions, where the procedure is legal, appear to be as low as or lower than the rates for normal childbirth. Consequently, any interest of the State in protecting the woman from an inherently hazardous procedure, except when it would be equally dangerous for her to forgo it, has largely disappeared. **Of course, important state interests in the areas of health and medical standards do remain.** The State has a legitimate interest in seeing to it that abortion, like any other medical procedure, is performed under circumstances that insure maximum safety for the patient. This interest obviously extends at least to the performing physician and his staff, to the facilities involved, to the availability of after-care, and to adequate provision for any complication or emergency that might arise. The prevalence of high mortality rates at illegal "abortion mills" strengthens, rather than weakens, the State's interest in regulating the conditions under which abortions are performed. Moreover, the risk to the woman increases as her

---

[1] *Griswold v. Connecticut*

31

pregnancy continues. Thus, the State retains a definite interest in protecting the woman's own health and safety when an abortion is proposed at a late stage of pregnancy.

The third reason is the State's interest — some phrase it in terms of duty — in protecting prenatal life. Some of the argument for this justification rests on the theory that a new human life is present from the moment of conception. The State's interest and general obligation to protect life then extends, it is argued, to prenatal life. Only when the life of the pregnant mother herself is at stake, balanced against the life she carries within her, should the interest of the embryo or fetus not prevail. Logically, of course, a legitimate state interest in this area need not stand or fall on acceptance of the belief that life begins at conception or at some other point prior to live birth. In assessing the State's interest, recognition may be given to the less rigid claim that as long as at least potential life is involved, the State may assert interests beyond the protection of the pregnant woman alone...

The Constitution does not explicitly mention any right of privacy. In a line of decisions, however, going back perhaps as far as 1891,[2] the Court has recognized that a right of personal privacy, or a guarantee of certain areas or zones of privacy, does exist under the

------

[2] *Union Pacific R. Co. v. Botsford*

Constitution. In varying contexts, the Court or individual Justices have, indeed, found at least the roots of that right in the First, Fourth, Fifth Ninth Amendment, and Fourteenth Amendments.[3]

These decisions make it clear that only personal rights that can be deemed "fundamental" or "implicit in the concept of ordered liberty,"[4] are included in this guarantee of personal privacy. They also make it clear that the right has some extension to activities relating to marriage, procreation, contraception, family relationships, and childrearing and education.[5]

This right of privacy, whether it be founded in the Fourteenth Amendment's concept of personal liberty and restrictions upon state action, as we feel it is, or, as the District Court determined, in the Ninth Amendment's reservation of rights to the people, is broad enough to encompass a woman's decision whether or not to terminate her pregnancy. The detriment that the State would impose upon the pregnant woman by denying this choice altogether is apparent. Specific and direct harm medically

---

[3] *Stanley v. Georgia; Terry v. Ohio; Katz v. United States; and Meyer v. Nebraska*

[4] *Palko v. Connecticut* (1937)

[5] *Loving v. Virginia; Skinner v. Oklahoma; Eisenstadt v. Bairdx; Prince v. Massachusetts; Pierce v. Society of Sisters;* and *Meyer v. Nebraska*

diagnosable even in early pregnancy may be involved. Maternity, or additional offspring, may force upon the woman a distressful life and future. Psychological harm may be imminent. Mental and physical health may be taxed by child care. There is also the distress, for all concerned, associated with the unwanted child, and there is the problem of bringing a child into a family already unable, psychologically and otherwise, to care for it. In other cases, as in this one, the additional difficulties and continuing stigma of unwed motherhood may be involved. All these are factors the woman and her responsible physician necessarily will consider in consultation.

On the basis of elements such as these, **appellant...argue[s] that the woman's right is absolute and that she is entitled to terminate her pregnancy at whatever time, in whatever way, and for whatever reason she alone chooses. With this we do not agree...As noted above, a State may properly assert important interests in safeguarding health, in maintaining medical standards, and in protecting potential life. At some point in pregnancy, these respective interests become sufficiently compelling to sustain regulation of the factors that govern the abortion decision. The privacy right involved, therefore, cannot be said to be absolute.** In fact, it is not clear to us that the claim asserted by some...that one has an unlimited right to do with one's body as one pleases bears a close relationship to the right of privacy previously articulated in the Court's decisions. The Court has refused to recognize an unlimited right of this kind in the past.[6]

We, therefore, conclude that the right of personal privacy includes the abortion decision, but that this right is not unqualified, and must be considered against important state interests in regulation...

Where certain "fundamental rights" are involved, the Court has held that regulation limiting these rights may be justified only by a "compelling state interest,"[7] and that legislative enactments must be narrowly drawn to express only the legitimate state interests at stake.[8] ...

A. The appellee...argue[s] that the fetus is a "person" within the language and meaning of the Fourteenth Amendment. In support of this, they outline at length and in detail the well known facts of fetal development. If this suggestion of personhood is established, the appellant's case, of course, collapses, for the fetus' right to life would then be guaranteed specifically by the Amendment. The appellant conceded as much on reargument. On the other hand, the appellee conceded on reargument that no case could be cited that holds

---

[6] *Jacobson v. Massachusetts* (1905) (vaccination); *Buck v. Bell* (1927) (sterilization)

[7] *Kramer v. Union Free School District* (1969)

[8] *Griswold v. Connecticut*

that a fetus is a person within the meaning of the Fourteenth Amendment.

The Constitution does not define "person" in so many words…But in nearly all these instances, the use of the word is such that it has application only post-natally. None indicates, with any assurance, that it has any possible pre-natal application.

All this…persuades us that the word "person," as used in the Fourteenth Amendment, does not include the unborn…

B. **The pregnant woman cannot be isolated in her privacy. She carries an embryo and, later, a fetus, if one accepts the medical definitions of the developing young in the human uterus. The situation therefore is inherently different from marital intimacy, or bedroom possession of obscene material, or marriage, or procreation, or education.**[9] As we have intimated above, it is reasonable and appropriate for a State to decide that, at some point in time another interest, that of health of the mother or that of potential human life, becomes significantly involved. The woman's privacy is no longer sole and any right of privacy she possesses must be measured accordingly.

Texas urges that, apart from the Fourteenth Amendment, life begins at conception and is present

---

[9] …With which *Eisenstadt* and *Griswold, Stanley, Loving, Skinner,* and *Pierce* and *Meyer* were respectively concerned.

throughout pregnancy, and that, therefore, the State has a compelling interest in protecting that life from and after conception. We need not resolve the difficult question of when life begins. When those trained in the respective disciplines of medicine, philosophy, and theology are unable to arrive at any consensus, the judiciary, at this point in the development of man's knowledge, is not in a position to speculate as to the answer.

It should be sufficient to note briefly the wide divergence of thinking on this most sensitive and difficult question...As we have noted, the common law found greater significance in quickening. Physicians and their scientific colleagues have regarded that event with less interest and have tended to focus either upon conception, upon live birth, or upon the interim point at which the fetus becomes "viable," that is, potentially able to live outside the mother's womb, albeit with artificial aid. Viability is usually placed at about seven months (28 weeks) but may occur earlier, even at 24 weeks...

[W]e do not agree that, by adopting one theory of life, Texas may override the rights of the pregnant woman that are at stake. We repeat, however, that the State does have an important and legitimate interest in preserving and protecting the health of the pregnant woman,...and that it has still another important and legitimate interest in protecting the potentiality of human life. These interests are separate and distinct. Each grows in substantiality as the woman approaches term and, at a point during pregnancy, each becomes "compelling."

With respect to the State's important and legitimate interest in the health of the mother, the "compelling" point, in the light of present medical knowledge, is at approximately the end of the first trimester. This is so because of the now-established medical fact, that, until the end of the first trimester mortality in abortion may be less than mortality in normal childbirth. It follows that, from and after this point, a State may regulate the abortion procedure to the extent that the regulation reasonably relates to the preservation and protection of maternal health. Examples of permissible state regulation in this area are requirements as to the qualifications of the person who is to perform the abortion; as to the licensure of that person; as to the facility in which the procedure is to be performed...as to the licensing of the facility; and the like.

This means, on the other hand, that, for the period of pregnancy prior to this "compelling" point, the attending physician, in consultation with his patient, is free to determine, without regulation by the State, that, in his medical judgment, the patient's pregnancy should be terminated. If that decision is reached, the judgment may be effectuated by an abortion free of interference by the State.

With respect to the State's important and legitimate interest in potential life, the

"compelling" point is at viability. This is so because the fetus then presumably has the capability of meaningful life outside the mother's womb. State regulation protective of fetal life after viability thus has both logical and biological justifications. If the State is interested in protecting fetal life after viability, it may go so far as to proscribe abortion during that period, except when it is necessary to preserve the life or health of the mother.

Measured against these standards, Article 1196 of the Texas Penal Code, in restricting legal abortions to those "procured or attempted by medical advice for the purpose of saving the life of the mother," sweeps too broadly. The statute makes no distinction between abortions performed early in pregnancy and those performed later, and it limits to a single reason, "saving" the mother's life, the legal justification for the procedure. The statute, therefore, cannot survive the constitutional attack made upon it here…

Justice Blackmun's Summary
From *Roe v. Wade* Opinion

1. A state criminal abortion statute of the current Texas type, that excepts from criminality only a lifesaving procedure on behalf of the mother, without regard to pregnancy stage and without recognition of the other interests involved, is violative of the Due Process Clause of the Fourteenth Amendment.

(a) For the stage prior to approximately the end of the first trimester, the abortion decision and its effectuation must be left to the medical judgment of the pregnant woman's attending physician.

(b) For the stage subsequent to approximately the end of the first trimester, the State, in promoting its interest in the health of the mother, may, if it chooses, regulate the abortion procedure in ways that are reasonably related to maternal health.

(c) For the stage subsequent to viability, the State in promoting its interest in the potentiality of human life may, if it chooses, regulate, and even proscribe, abortion except where it is necessary, in appropriate medical judgment, for the preservation of the life or health of the mother.

2. The State may define the term "physician," as it has been employed in the preceding paragraphs…to mean only a physician currently licensed by the State, and may proscribe any abortion by a person who is not a physician as so defined…

The decision leaves the State free to place increasing restrictions on abortion as the period of pregnancy lengthens, so long as those restrictions are tailored to the recognized state interests. The decision vindicates the right of the physician to administer medical treatment according to his professional judgment up to the points where important state interests provide compelling justifications for intervention. Up to those points, the abortion decision in all its aspects is inherently, and primarily, a medical decision, and basic responsibility for it must rest with the physician. If an individual practitioner abuses the privilege of exercising proper medical judgment, the usual remedies, judicial and intra-professional, are available.

Justice Stewart's Concurring Opinion In *Roe v. Wade*

"In a Constitution for a free people, there can be no doubt that the meaning of 'liberty' must be broad indeed."[10] The Constitution nowhere mentions a specific right of personal choice in matters of marriage and family life, but the "liberty" protected by the Due Process Clause of the Fourteenth Amendment covers more than those freedoms explicitly named in the Bill of Rights.

As Mr. Justice Harlan once wrote: "[T]he full scope of the liberty guaranteed by the Due Process Clause cannot be found in or limited by the precise terms of the specific guarantees elsewhere provided in the Constitution. This "liberty" is not a series of isolated points pricked out in terms of the taking of property; the freedom of speech, press, and religion; the right to keep and bear arms; the freedom from unreasonable searches and seizures; and so on. It is a rational continuum which, broadly speaking, includes a freedom from all substantial arbitrary impositions and purposeless restraints . . . and which also recognizes, ...that certain interests require particularly careful scrutiny of the state needs asserted to justify their abridgment.

In the words of Mr. Justice Frankfurter: "Great concepts like...'liberty'...were purposely left to

---

[10] *Board of Regents v. Roth*

gather meaning from experience. For they relate to the whole domain of social and economic fact, and the statesmen who founded this Nation knew too well that only a stagnant society remains unchanged...

As recently as last Term[11] we recognized the right of the *individual,* married or single, to be free from unwarranted governmental intrusion into matters so fundamentally affecting a person as the decision whether to bear or beget a child. That right necessarily includes the right of a woman to decide whether or not to terminate her pregnancy.

Certainly the interests of a woman in giving of her physical and emotional self during pregnancy and the interests that will be affected throughout her life by the birth and raising of a child are of a far greater degree of significance and personal intimacy than the right to send a child to private school or the right to teach a foreign language.[12]

Clearly, therefore, the Court today is correct in holding that the right asserted by Jane Roe is embraced within the personal liberty protected by the Due Process Clause of the Fourteenth Amendment.

---

[11] In *Eisenstadt v. Baird* (a case dealing with the use of contraception)

[12] *Pierce v. Society of Sisters* (1925); *Meyer v. Nebraska* (1923)

It is evident that the Texas abortion statute infringes that right directly. Indeed, it is difficult to imagine a more complete abridgment of a constitutional freedom than that worked by the inflexible criminal statute now in force in Texas...

The asserted state interests are protection of the health and safety of the pregnant woman, and protection of the potential future human life within her. These are legitimate objectives, amply sufficient to permit a State to regulate abortions as it does other surgical procedures, and perhaps sufficient to permit a State to regulate abortions more stringently, or even to prohibit them in the late stages of pregnancy. But such legislation is not before us, and I think the Court today has thoroughly demonstrated that these state interests cannot constitutionally support the broad abridgment of personal liberty worked by the existing Texas law.

Accordingly, I join the Court's opinion holding that that law is invalid under the Due Process Clause of the Fourteenth Amendment.

Dissenting Opinion by Mr. Justice Rehnquist in *Roe v. Wade*

The Court's opinion brings to the decision of this troubling question both extensive historical fact and a wealth of legal scholarship. While the opinion thus commands my respect, I find myself nonetheless in fundamental disagreement with those parts of it that invalidate the Texas statute in question, and therefore dissent.

...I have difficulty in concluding, as the Court does, that the right of "privacy" is involved in this case. Texas, by the statute here challenged, bars the performance of a medical abortion by a licensed physician on a plaintiff such as Roe. **A transaction resulting in an operation such as this is not "private" in the ordinary usage of that word. Nor is the "privacy" that the Court finds here even a distant relative of the freedom from searches and seizures protected by the Fourth Amendment to the Constitution, which the Court has referred to as embodying a right to privacy.**[13]

...If the Texas statute were to prohibit an abortion even where the mother's life is in jeopardy, I have little doubt that such a statute would lack a rational relation to a valid state objective under the test stated in *Williamson*.[14] But the Court's sweeping

---

[13] *Katz v. United States* (1967)
[14] *Williamson v. Lee Optical of Oklahoma, Inc.* (1955)

45

invalidation of any restrictions on abortion during the first trimester is impossible to justify under that standard, and the conscious weighing of competing factors that the Court's opinion apparently substitutes for the established test is far more appropriate to a legislative judgment than to a judicial one.

...[T]he Court adds a new wrinkle to this [compelling state interest] test by transposing it from the legal considerations associated with the Equal Protection Clause of the Fourteenth Amendment to this case arising under the Due Process Clause of the Fourteenth Amendment. **Unless I misapprehend the consequences of this transplanting of the "compelling state interest test," the Court's opinion will accomplish the seemingly impossible feat of leaving this area of the law more confused than it found it.**

...The decision here to break pregnancy into three distinct terms and to outline the permissible restrictions the State may impose in each one, for example, partakes more of judicial legislation than it does of a determination of the intent of the drafters of the Fourteenth Amendment.

The fact that a majority of the States reflecting, after all, the majority sentiment in those States, have had restrictions on abortions for at least a century is a strong indication, it seems to me, that the asserted right to an abortion is not "so rooted in the traditions and

conscience of our people as to be ranked as fundamental."[15] Even today, when society's views on abortion are changing, the very existence of the debate is evidence that the "right" to an abortion is not so universally accepted as the appellant would have us believe.

To reach its result, the Court necessarily has had to find within the scope of the Fourteenth Amendment a right that was apparently completely unknown to the drafters of the Amendment. As early as 1821, the first state law dealing directly with abortion was enacted by the Connecticut Legislature. By the time of the adoption of the Fourteenth Amendment in 1868, there were at least 36 laws enacted by state or territorial legislatures limiting abortion. While many States have amended or updated their laws, 21 of the laws on the books in 1868 remain in effect today. Indeed, the Texas statute struck down today was, as the majority notes, first enacted in 1857, and "has remained substantially unchanged to the present time."

There apparently was no question concerning the validity of this provision or of any of the other state statutes when the Fourteenth Amendment was adopted. The only conclusion possible from this history is that the drafters did not intend to have the Fourteenth Amendment withdraw from the States the power to legislate with respect to this matter.

---

[15] *Snyder v. Massachusetts* (1934)

Even if one were to agree that the case that the Court decides were here, and that the enunciation of the substantive constitutional law in the Court's opinion were proper, the actual disposition of the case by the Court is still difficult to justify. The Texas statute is struck down in toto, even though the Court apparently concedes that, at later periods of pregnancy Texas might impose these self-same statutory limitations on abortion. My understanding of past practice is that a statute found to be invalid as applied to a particular plaintiff, but not unconstitutional as a whole, is not simply "struck down" but is, instead, declared unconstitutional as applied to the fact situation before the Court.[16] For all of the foregoing reasons, I respectfully dissent.

---

[16] *Yick Wo v. Hopkins* (1886); *Street v. New York* (1969)

Dissenting Opinion by Mr. Justice White In *Roe v. Wade*

At the heart of the controversy in these cases are those recurring pregnancies that pose no danger whatsoever to the life or health of the mother but are, nevertheless, unwanted for any one or more of a variety of reasons — convenience, family planning, economics, dislike of children, the embarrassment of illegitimacy, etc. The common claim before us is that, for any one of such reasons, or for no reason at all, and without asserting or claiming any threat to life or health, any woman is entitled to an abortion at her request if she is able to find a medical advisor willing to undertake the procedure.

The Court, for the most part, sustains this position...

With all due respect, I dissent. I find nothing in the language or history of the Constitution to support the Court's judgment. The Court simply fashions and announces a new constitutional right for pregnant mothers and, with scarcely any reason or authority for its action, invests that right with sufficient substance to override most existing state abortion statutes. The upshot is that the people and the legislatures of the 50 States are constitutionally dissentitled to weigh the relative importance of the continued existence and development of the fetus, on the one hand, against a spectrum of possible impacts on the mother, on the other hand. As an exercise of raw judicial power, the Court perhaps has authority to do what it does today; but, in my view, its judgment is an improvident and extravagant exercise of the power of judicial review that the Constitution extends to this Court.

...In a sensitive area such as this, involving as it does issues over which reasonable men may easily and heatedly differ, I cannot accept the Court's exercise of its clear power of choice by interposing a constitutional barrier to state efforts to protect human life and by investing mothers and doctors with the constitutionally protected right to exterminate it. This issue...should be left with the people and to the political processes the people have devised to govern their affairs. It is my view, therefore, that the Texas statute is not constitutionally infirm because it denies abortions to those who seek to serve only their convenience, rather than to protect their life or health...

Doe v. Bolton

Mary Doe

v.
Arthur K. Bolton,
Attorney General of Georgia, et al.

Argued December 13, 1971
Reargued October 11, 1972
Decided January 22, 1973

Primary Case Opinions
Majority: Blackmun, joined by Burger,
Douglas, Brennan, Steward,
Marshall, Powell

Dissent: White, joined by Rehnquist

Mr. Justice Blackmun's Majority Opinion In *Doe v. Bolton*

In this appeal, the criminal abortion statutes recently enacted in Georgia are challenged on constitutional grounds. In *Roe v. Wade,* we today have struck down, as constitutionally defective, the Texas criminal abortion statutes that are representative of provisions long in effect in a majority of our States. The Georgia legislation, however, is different and merits separate consideration…

As the appellants acknowledge, [Georgia's] 1968 statutes are patterned upon the American Law Institute's Model Penal Code. The ALI proposal has served as the model for recent legislation in approximately one-fourth of our States. The new Georgia provisions replaced statutory law that had been in effect for more than 90 years…

[The new statutes] with a referenced exception, make abortion a crime, and provide that a person convicted of that crime shall be punished by imprisonment for not less than one nor more than 10 years…[T]he exception…makes noncriminal an abortion "performed by a physician duly licensed" in Georgia when "based upon his best clinical judgment...an abortion is necessary because:

"(1) A continuation of the pregnancy would endanger the life of the pregnant woman or would seriously and permanently injure her health; or

"(2) The fetus would very likely be born with a grave, permanent, and irremediable mental or physical defect; or

"(3) The pregnancy resulted from forcible or statutory rape."

[The statute] also requires...that, for an abortion to be authorized or performed as a noncriminal procedure, additional conditions must be fulfilled. These are ... (2) residence of the woman in Georgia; (3) ...written concurrence in that judgment by at least two other Georgia-licensed physicians, based upon their separate personal medical examinations of the woman; (4) performance of the abortion in a hospital licensed by the State Board of Health and also accredited by the Joint Commission on Accreditation of Hospitals; (5) advance approval by an abortion committee...; (6) certifications in a rape situation; and...(9) maintenance and confidentiality of records. There is a provision for judicial determination of the legality of a proposed abortion ...and for expeditious hearing of that petition. There is also a provision giving a hospital the right not to admit an abortion patient and giving any physician and any hospital employee or staff member the right, on moral or religious grounds, not to participate in the procedure.

On April 16, 1970, Mary Doe, 23 other individuals (nine described as Georgia-licensed physicians, seven as nurses registered in the State, five as clergymen, and two as social workers), and two nonprofit Georgia corporations that advocate abortion reform instituted this federal action in the Northern District of Georgia…The plaintiffs sought a declaratory judgment that the Georgia abortion statutes were unconstitutional in their entirety…

Mary Doe alleged:

(1) She was a 22-year-old Georgia citizen, married, and nine weeks pregnant. She had three living children. The two older ones had been placed in a foster home because of Doe's poverty and inability to care for them. The youngest, born July 19, 1969, had been placed for adoption. Her husband had recently abandoned her and she was forced to live with her indigent parents and their eight children. She and her husband, however, had become reconciled. He was a construction worker employed only sporadically. She had been a mental patient at the State Hospital. She had been advised that an abortion could be performed on her with less danger to her health than if she gave birth to the child she was carrying. She would be unable to care for or support the new child.

(2) On March 25, 1970, she applied to the Abortion Committee of Grady Memorial Hospital, Atlanta, for a therapeutic abortion. Her application was denied 16 days later, on April 10, when she was eight weeks pregnant, on the ground that her situation was not one described in [the statute].

(3) Because her application was denied, she was forced either to relinquish "her right to decide when and how many children she will bear" or to seek an abortion that was illegal under the Georgia statutes. This invaded her rights of privacy and liberty in matters related to family, marriage, and sex, and deprived her of the right to choose whether to bear children. This was a violation of rights guaranteed her by the First, Fourth, Fifth, Ninth, and Fourteenth Amendments. The statutes also denied her equal protection and procedural due process and, because they were unconstitutionally vague, deterred hospitals and doctors from performing abortions. She sued "on her own behalf and on behalf of all others similarly situated."

…[T]he court concluded that the limitation in the Georgia statute of the "number of reasons for which an abortion may be sought," improperly restricted Doe's rights of privacy articulated in *Griswold v. Connecticut* (1965), and of "personal liberty," both of which it thought "broad enough to include the decision to abort a pregnancy." As a consequence, the court held invalid those portions of [the statute] limiting legal abortions to the three situations specified…The court, however, held that Georgia's interest in protection of health, and the existence of a "*potential* of independent human existence" (emphasis in original), justified state regulation of "the manner of performance as well as the quality of the final decision to abort," and it refused to strike down the other provisions of the statutes...

The appellants attack on several grounds those portions of the Georgia abortion statutes that remain...: undue restriction of a right to personal and marital privacy; vagueness; deprivation of substantive and procedural due process; improper restriction to Georgia residents; and denial of equal protection.

Roe v. Wade sets forth our conclusion that a pregnant woman does not have an absolute constitutional right to an abortion on her demand. What is said there is applicable here and need not be repeated...

Appellants then argue that the statutes do not adequately protect the woman's right. This is so because it would be physically and emotionally damaging to Doe to bring a child into her poor, "fatherless" family, and because advances in medicine and medical techniques have made it safer for a woman to have a medically induced abortion than for her to bear a child. **Thus, "a statute that requires a woman to carry an unwanted pregnancy to term infringes not only on a fundamental right of privacy but on the right to life itself."**

Appellants argue that [this] section of the Georgia statutes...is unconstitutionally vague. This argument centers on the proposition that, with the District Court's having struck down the statutorily specified reasons, it still remains a crime for a physician to perform an abortion except when, as [it] reads, it is "based upon his best clinical judgment that an abortion is necessary." The appellants contend that the word "necessary" does not warn the physician of what conduct is proscribed; that the statute is wholly without objective standards and is subject to diverse interpretation; and that doctors will choose to err on the side of caution and will be arbitrary...

The vagueness argument is set at rest by the decision in *United States v. Vuitch* (1971), where the issue was raised with respect to a District of Columbia statute making abortions criminal "unless the same were done as necessary for the preservation of the mother's life or health and under the direction of a competent licensed practitioner of medicine." That statute has been construed to bear upon psychological as well as physical well-being. This being so, the Court concluded that the term "health" presented no problem of vagueness. "Indeed, whether a particular operation is necessary for a patient's physical or mental health is a judgment that physicians are obviously called upon to make routinely whenever surgery is considered." This conclusion is equally applicable here. Whether, in the words of the Georgia statute, "an abortion is necessary" is a professional judgment that the Georgia physician will be called upon to make routinely.

We agree with the District Court, that the medical judgment may be exercised in the light of all factors—physical, emotional, psychological, familial, and the woman's age—relevant to the wellbeing of the patient. All these factors may relate to health. This allows the attending physician the room he needs to make his best medical judgment. And it is room that operates for the benefit, not the disadvantage, of the pregnant woman.

The appellants next argue that the District Court should have declared unconstitutional three procedural demands of the Georgia statute: (1) that the abortion be performed in a hospital accredited by the Joint Commission on Accreditation of Hospitals: (2) that the procedure be approved by the hospital staff abortion committee; and (3) that the performing physician's judgment be confirmed by the independent examinations of the patient by two other licensed physicians. The appellants attack these provisions not only on the ground that they unduly restrict the woman's right of privacy, but also on procedural due process and equal protection grounds. The physician-appellants also argue that, by subjecting a doctor's individual medical judgment to committee approval and to confirming consultations, the statute impermissibly restricts the physician's right to practice his profession and deprives him of due process.

JCAH accreditation. The Joint Commission on Accreditation of Hospitals is an organization without governmental sponsorship or overtones. No question whatever is raised concerning the integrity of the organization or the high purpose of the accreditation process. That process, however, has to do with hospital standards generally and has no present particularized concern with abortion as a medical or surgical procedure. In Georgia, there is no restriction on the performance of non-abortion surgery in a hospital not yet accredited by the JCAH so long as other requirements imposed by the State, such as licensing of the hospital and of the operating surgeon, are met...We hold that the JCAH-accreditation requirement does not withstand constitutional scrutiny in the present context. It is a requirement that simply is not "based on differences that are reasonably related to the purposes of the Act in which it is found."[17]

This is not to say that Georgia may not or should not, from and after the end of the first trimester, adopt standards for licensing all facilities where abortions may be performed so long as those standards are legitimately related to the objective the State seeks to accomplish...Appellants and various *amici* have presented us with a mass of data purporting to demonstrate that some facilities other than hospitals are entirely adequate to perform

---

[17] *Morey v. Doud* (1957)

abortions if they possess these qualifications. The State, on the other hand, has not presented persuasive data to show that only hospitals meet its acknowledged interest in insuring the quality of the operation and the full protection of the patient. We feel compelled to agree with appellants that the State must show more than it has in order to prove that only the full resources of a licensed hospital, rather than those of some other appropriately licensed institution, satisfy these health interests. We hold that the hospital requirement of the Georgia law, because it fails to exclude the first trimester of pregnancy, is also invalid...

Committee approval. The second aspect of the appellants' procedural attack relates to the hospital abortion committee and to the pregnant woman's asserted lack of access to that committee...Appellants attack the discretion the statute leaves to the committee. The most concrete argument they advance is their suggestion that it is still a badge of infamy "in many minds" to bear an illegitimate child, and that the Georgia system enables the committee members' personal views as to extramarital sex relations, and punishment therefor, to govern their decisions. This approach obviously is one founded on suspicion and one that discloses a lack of confidence in the integrity of physicians. To say that physicians will be guided in their hospital committee decisions by their predilections on extramarital sex unduly narrows the issue to pregnancy outside marriage. (Doe's own situation did not involve extramarital sex and its product.)

...It is perhaps worth noting that the abortion committee has a function of its own. It is a committee of the hospital and it is composed of members of the institution's medical staff...The committee's function is protective. It enables the hospital appropriately to be advised that its posture and activities are in accord with legal requirements. It is to be remembered that the hospital is an entity and that it, too, has legal rights and legal obligations.

Saying all this, however, does not settle the issue of the constitutional propriety of the committee requirement...With regard to the protection of potential life, the medical judgment is already completed prior to the committee stage, and review by a committee once removed from diagnosis is basically redundant. We are not cited to any other surgical procedure made subject to committee approval as a matter of state criminal law. The woman's right to receive medical care in accordance with her licensed physician's best judgment and the physician's right to administer it are substantially limited by this statutorily imposed overview. **And the hospital itself is otherwise fully protected. The hospital is free not to admit a patient for an abortion. It is even free not to have an abortion committee. Further, a physician or any other employee has the right to refrain, for moral or**

religious reasons, from participating in the abortion procedure. These provisions obviously are in the statute in order to afford appropriate protection to the individual and to the denominational hospital...

We conclude that the interposition of the hospital abortion committee is unduly restrictive of the patient's rights and needs that, at this point, have already been medically delineated and substantiated by her personal physician. To ask more serves neither the hospital nor the State.

Two-doctor concurrence. The third aspect of the appellants' attack centers on the "time and availability of adequate medical facilities and personnel." It is said that the system imposes substantial and irrational roadblocks and "is patently unsuited" to prompt determination of the abortion decision. Time, of course, is critical in abortion. Risks during the first trimester of pregnancy are admittedly lower than during later months...We conclude that this provision, too, must fall...

The appellants attack the residency requirement of the Georgia law, as violative of the right to travel stressed in *Shapiro v. Thompson* (1969) and other cases. A requirement of this kind, of course, could be deemed to have some relationship to the availability of post-procedure medical care for the aborted patient.

Nevertheless, we do not uphold the constitutionality of the residence requirement. It is not based on any policy of preserving state-supported facilities for Georgia residents, for the bar also applies to private hospitals and to privately retained physicians. There is no intimation, either, that Georgia facilities are utilized to capacity in caring for Georgia residents. Just as the Privileges and Immunities Clause, Constitution Article IV, Section 2, protects persons who enter other States to ply their trade,[18] so must it protect persons who enter Georgia seeking the medical services that are available there. A contrary holding would mean that a State could limit to its own residents the general medical care available within its borders. This we could not approve…

In summary, we hold that the JCAH-accredited hospital provision and the requirements as to approval by the hospital abortion committee, as to confirmation by two independent physicians, and as to residence in Georgia are all violative of the Fourteenth Amendment…

---

[18] *Ward v. Maryland* (1871); *Blake v. McClung* (1898)

Mr. Justice Douglas, Concurring
In *Doe v. Bolton*

While I join the opinion of the Court, I add a few words.

The questions presented in the present cases go far beyond the issues of vagueness, which we considered in *United States v. Vuitch*. They involve the right of privacy, one aspect of which we considered in *Griswold v. Connecticut*, when we held that various guarantees in the Bill of Rights create zones of privacy.

The *Griswold* case involved a law forbidding the use of contraceptives. We held that law as applied to married people unconstitutional: **"We deal with a right of privacy older than the Bill of Rights-- older than our political parties, older than our school system. Marriage is a coming together for better or for worse, hopefully enduring, and intimate to the degree of being sacred."**

…The Ninth Amendment obviously does not create federally enforceable rights. It merely says, "The enumeration in the Constitution, of certain rights, shall not be construed to deny or disparage others retained by the people." But a catalogue of these rights includes customary, traditional, and time-honored rights, amenities, privileges, and immunities that come within the sweep of "the Blessings of Liberty" mentioned in the preamble to the Constitution. Many of them, in my view, come

64

within the meaning of the term "liberty" as used in the Fourteenth Amendment.

First is the autonomous control over the development and expression of one's intellect, interests, tastes, and personality.

These are rights protected by the First Amendment and, in my view, they are absolute, permitting of no exceptions. The Free Exercise Clause of the First Amendment is one facet of this constitutional right. **The right to remain silent as respects one's own beliefs, is protected by the First and the Fifth**...All of these aspects of the right of privacy are rights "retained by the people" in the meaning of the Ninth Amendment.

Second is freedom of choice in the basic decisions of one's life respecting marriage, divorce, procreation, contraception, and the education and upbringing of children.

These rights, unlike those protected by the First Amendment, are subject to some control by the police power. Thus, the Fourth Amendment speaks only of "unreasonable searches and seizures" and of "probable cause." **These rights are "fundamental," and we have held that in order to support legislative action the statute must be narrowly and precisely drawn and that a "compelling state interest" must be shown in support of the limitation.**

The liberty to marry a person of one's own choosing; the right of procreation; the liberty to direct the education of one's children; and the privacy of the marital relation, are in this category...If the right of privacy means anything, it is the right of the *individual*, married or single, to be free from unwarranted governmental intrusion into matters so fundamentally affecting a person as the decision whether to bear or beget a child."

This right of privacy was called by Mr. Justice Brandeis the right "to be let alone."[19] **That right includes the privilege of an individual to plan his own affairs, for, "'outside areas of plainly harmful conduct, every American is left to shape his own life as he thinks best, do what he pleases, go where he pleases.'"[20]**

Third is the freedom to care for one's health and person, freedom from bodily restraint or compulsion, freedom to walk, stroll, or loaf.

These rights, though fundamental, are likewise subject to regulation on a showing of "compelling state interest." We stated in *Papachristou v. City of Jacksonville*, that walking, strolling, and wandering "are historically part of the amenities of life as we have known them." **As stated in *Jacobson v. Massachusetts*: "There is, of course, a sphere within which the individual may assert the supremacy of his own will and rightfully dispute the authority of any human government,**

---

[19] *Olmstead v. United States* (dissenting opinion)
[20] *Kent v. Dulles*

especially of any free government existing under a written constitution, to interfere with the exercise of that will."

…In *Terry v. Ohio*, the Court, in speaking of the Fourth Amendment stated, "This inestimable right of personal security belongs as much to the citizen on the streets of our cities as to the homeowner closeted in his study to dispose of his secret affairs." *Katz v. United States* emphasizes that the Fourth Amendment "protects individual privacy against certain kinds of governmental intrusion."

In ***Meyer v. Nebraska*, the Court said: "Without doubt, [liberty] denotes not merely freedom from bodily restraint but also the right of the individual to contract, to engage in any of the common occupations of life, to acquire useful knowledge, to marry, establish a home and bring up children, to worship God according to the dictates of his own conscience, and generally to enjoy those privileges long recognized at common law as essential to the orderly pursuit of happiness by free men."**

The Georgia statute is at war with the clear message of these cases--that a woman is free to make the basic decision whether to bear an unwanted child. Elaborate argument is hardly necessary to demonstrate that childbirth may deprive a woman of her preferred lifestyle and force upon her a radically different and undesired future. For example, rejected applicants under the Georgia statute are required to endure the discomforts of pregnancy; to incur the pain, higher mortality rate, and aftereffects of childbirth; to abandon educational plans; to sustain loss of income; to forgo the satisfactions of careers; to tax further mental and physical health in providing child care; and, in some cases, to bear the lifelong stigma of unwed motherhood, a badge which may haunt, if not deter, later legitimate family relationships.

Such reasoning is, however, only the beginning of the problem. The State has interests to protect...While childbirth endangers the lives of some women, voluntary abortion at any time and place regardless of medical standards would impinge on a rightful concern of society. **The woman's health is part of that concern; as is the life of the fetus after quickening. These concerns justify the State in treating the procedure as a medical one.**

...The vicissitudes of life produce pregnancies which may be unwanted, or which may impair "health" in the broad *Vuitch* sense of the term, or which may imperil the life of the mother, or which in the full setting of the case may create such suffering, dislocations, misery, or tragedy as to make an early abortion the only civilized step to take. These hardships may be properly embraced in the "health" factor of the mother as appraised by a person of insight. Or they may be part of a broader medical judgment based on what is "appropriate" in a given case, though perhaps not "necessary" in a strict sense.

The "liberty" of the mother, though rooted as it is in the Constitution, may be qualified by the State for the reasons we have stated. But where fundamental personal rights and liberties are involved, the corrective legislation must be "narrowly drawn to prevent the supposed evil,"[21] and not be dealt with in an "unlimited and indiscriminate" manner.[22] **Unless regulatory measures are so confined and are addressed to the specific areas of compelling legislative concern, the police power would become the great leveler of constitutional rights and liberties.**

There is no doubt that the State may require abortions to be performed by qualified medical personnel. The legitimate objective of preserving the mother's health clearly supports such laws. Their impact upon the woman's privacy is minimal. But the Georgia statute outlaws virtually all such operations--even in the earliest stages of pregnancy. In light of modern medical evidence suggesting that an early abortion is safer healthwise than childbirth itself, it cannot be seriously urged that so comprehensive a ban is aimed at protecting the woman's health. Rather, this expansive proscription of all abortions

---

[21] *Cantwell v. Connecticut*
[22] *Shelton v. Tucker*

along the temporal spectrum can rest only on a public goal of preserving both embryonic and fetal life...

As Mr. Justice Clark has said: "To say that life is present at conception is to give recognition to the potential, rather than the actual. The unfertilized egg has life, and if fertilized, it takes on human proportions. But the law deals in reality, not obscurity--the known rather than the unknown. When sperm meets egg life may eventually form, but quite often it does not. The law does not deal in speculation. The phenomenon of life takes time to develop, and until it is actually present, it cannot be destroyed. Its interruption prior to formation would hardly be homicide, and as we have seen, society does not regard it as such. The rites of Baptism are not performed and death certificates are not required when a miscarriage occurs. No prosecutor has ever returned a murder indictment charging the taking of the life of a fetus. This would not be the case if the fetus constituted human life."

In summary, the enactment is overbroad... because it equates the value of embryonic life immediately after conception with the worth of life immediately before birth...

The right of privacy--the right to care for one's health and person and to seek out a physician of one's own choice protected by the Fourteenth Amendment--becomes only a matter of theory, not a reality, when a multiple-

physician-approval system is mandated by the State.

The State licenses a physician. If he is derelict or faithless, the procedures available to punish him or to deprive him of his license are well known. He is entitled to procedural due process before professional disciplinary sanctions may be imposed. Crucial here, however, is state-imposed control over the medical decision whether pregnancy should be interrupted...This is a total destruction of the right of privacy between physician and patient and the intimacy of relation which that entails.

The right to seek advice on one's health and the right to place reliance on the physician of one's choice are basic to Fourteenth Amendment values... Georgia has constitutional warrant in treating abortion as a medical problem. To protect the woman's right of privacy, however, the control must be through the physician of her choice and the standards set for his performance...

In short, I agree with the Court that endangering the life of the woman or seriously and permanently injuring her health are standards too narrow for the right of privacy that is at stake. I also agree that the superstructure of medical supervision which Georgia has erected violates the patient's right of privacy inherent in her choice of her own physician.

Mr. Justice White's Dissent
In *Doe v. Bolton*

At the heart of the controversy in these cases are those recurring pregnancies that pose no danger whatsoever to the life or health of the mother but are, nevertheless, unwanted for any one or more of a variety of reasons--convenience, family planning, economics, dislike of children, the embarrassment of illegitimacy, etc. **The common claim before us is that for any one of such reasons, or for no reason at all, and without asserting or claiming any threat to life or health, any woman is entitled to an abortion at her request if she is able to find a medical advisor willing to undertake the procedure.**

...With all due respect, I dissent. I find nothing in the language or history of the Constitution to support the Court's judgment.

...**The Court apparently values the convenience of the pregnant mother more than the continued existence and development of the life or potential life that she carries.** Whether or not I might agree with that marshaling of values, I can in no event join the Court's judgment because I find no constitutional warrant for imposing such an order of priorities on the people and legislatures of the States. **In a sensitive area such as this, involving as it does issues over which reasonable men may easily and heatedly differ, I cannot** accept the Court's exercise of its clear power of choice by interposing a constitutional barrier to state efforts to protect human life and by investing mothers and doctors with the constitutionally protected right to exterminate it. This issue, for the most part, should be left with the people and to the political processes the people have devised to govern their affairs.

...[B]ecause Georgia may constitutionally forbid abortions to putative mothers who, like the plaintiff in this case, do not fall within the reach...of its criminal code, I have no occasion...to consider the constitutionality of the procedural requirements of the Georgia statute as applied to those pregnancies posing substantial hazards to either life or health. I would reverse the judgment of the District Court in the Georgia case.

"And yet our opponents tell us not to interfere with abortion. They tell us not to impose our morality on those who wish to allow or participate in the taking of the life of infants before birth. Yet no one calls it imposing morality to prohibit the taking of life after a child is born. We're told about a woman's right to control her own body. But doesn't the unborn child have a higher right, and that is to life, liberty, and the pursuit of happiness?"

President Ronald Reagan
January 22, 1988

Planned Parenthood v. Casey

Planned Parenthood of Southeastern Pennsylvania, et al.

v.

Robert P. Casey, et al.

**Argued April 22, 1992
Decided June 29, 1992**

Case Opinions

Plurality: O'Connor, Kennedy, Souter

Concur/Dissent: Stevens

Concur/Dissent: Blackmun

**Concur/Dissent: Rehnquist, joined by
White Scalia, Thomas**

**Concur/Dissent: Scalia, joined by
Rehnquist, White, Thomas**

Lesson on Power and Function of the Supreme Court
(From the Majority Opinion of
Planned Parenthood v. Casey)

The examination of the conditions justifying the repudiation of Adkins by West Coast and Plessy by Brown is enough to suggest the terrible price that would have been paid if the Court had not overruled as it did. In the present cases, however...the terrible price would be paid for overruling. Our analysis would not be complete, however, without explaining why overruling Roe's central holding...would seriously weaken the Court's capacity to exercise the judicial power and to function as the Supreme Court of a Nation dedicated to the rule of law. To understand why this would be so, it is necessary to understand the source of this Court's authority, the conditions necessary for its preservation, and its relationship to the country's understanding of itself as a constitutional Republic.

The root of American governmental power is revealed most clearly in the instance of the power conferred by the Constitution upon the Judiciary of the United States, and specifically upon this Court. As Americans of each succeeding generation are rightly told, the Court cannot buy support for its decisions by spending money, and, except to a minor degree, it cannot independently coerce obedience to its decrees. **The Court's power lies, rather, in its** legitimacy, a product of substance and perception that shows itself in the people's acceptance of the Judiciary as fit to determine what the Nation's law means, and to declare what it demands.

The underlying substance of this legitimacy is of course the warrant for the Court's decisions in the Constitution and the lesser sources of legal principle on which the Court draws. That substance is expressed in the Court's opinions, and our contemporary understanding is such that a decision without principled justification would be no judicial act at all...The Court must take care to speak and act in ways that allow people to accept its decisions on the terms the Court claims for them, as grounded truly in principle, not as compromises with social and political pressures having, as such, no bearing on the principled choices that the Court is obliged to make. Thus, the Court's legitimacy depends on making legally principled decisions under circumstances in which their principled character is sufficiently plausible to be accepted by the Nation.

The need for principled action to be perceived as such is implicated to some degree whenever this, or any other appellate court, overrules a prior case. This is not to say, of course, that this Court cannot give a perfectly satisfactory explanation in most cases. People understand that some of the

Constitution's language is hard to fathom, and that the Court's Justices are sometimes able to perceive significant facts or to understand principles of law that eluded their predecessors and that justify departures from existing decisions. **However upsetting it may be to those most directly affected when one judicially derived rule replaces another, the country can accept some correction of error without necessarily questioning the legitimacy of the Court.**

In two circumstances, however, the Court would almost certainly fail to receive the benefit of the doubt in overruling prior cases. There is, first, a point beyond which frequent overruling would overtax the country's belief in the Court's good faith. **Despite the variety of reasons that may inform and justify a decision to overrule, we cannot forget that such a decision is usually perceived (and perceived correctly) as, at the least, a statement that a prior decision was wrong. There is a limit to the amount of error that can plausibly be imputed to prior Courts.** If that limit should be exceeded, disturbance of prior rulings would be taken as evidence that justifiable reexamination of principle had given way to drives for particular results in the short term. The legitimacy of the Court would fade with the frequency of its vacillation.

That first circumstance can be described as hypothetical; the second is to the point here and now.

Where, in the performance of its judicial duties, the Court decides a case in such a way as to resolve the sort of intensely divisive controversy reflected in Roe and those rare, comparable cases, its decision has a dimension that the resolution of the normal case does not carry. It is the dimension present whenever the Court's interpretation of the Constitution calls the contending sides of a national controversy to end their national division by accepting a common mandate rooted in the Constitution.

The Court is not asked to do this very often, having thus addressed the Nation only twice in our lifetime, in the decisions of Brown and Roe. But when the Court does act in this way, its decision requires an equally rare precedential force to counter the inevitable efforts to overturn it and to thwart its implementation. Some of those efforts may be mere unprincipled emotional reactions; others may proceed from principles worthy of profound respect. **But whatever the premises of opposition may be, only the most convincing justification under accepted standards of precedent could suffice to demonstrate that a later decision overruling the first was anything but a surrender to political pressure and an unjustified repudiation of the principle on which the Court staked its authority in the first instance. So to overrule under fire in the absence of the most compelling reason to reexamine a watershed decision would subvert** the Court's legitimacy beyond any serious question.

...Some cost will be paid by anyone who approves or implements a constitutional decision where it is unpopular, or who refuses to work to undermine the decision or to force its reversal. The price may be criticism or ostracism, or it may be violence. An extra price will be paid by those who themselves disapprove of the decision's results when viewed outside of constitutional terms, but who nevertheless struggle to accept it, because they respect the rule of law. To all those who will be so tested by following, the Court implicitly undertakes to remain steadfast, lest in the end a price be paid for nothing. The promise of constancy, once given, binds its maker for as long as the power to stand by the decision survives and the understanding of the issue has not changed so fundamentally as to render the commitment obsolete. **From the obligation of this promise, this Court cannot and should not assume any exemption when duty requires it to decide a case in conformance with the Constitution. A willing breach of it would be nothing less than a breach of faith, and no Court that broke its faith with the people could sensibly expect credit for principle in the decision by which it did that.**

It is true that diminished legitimacy may be restored, but only slowly...**Like the character of an individual, the legitimacy of the Court must be** earned over time. So, indeed, must be the character of a Nation of people who aspire to live according to the rule of law. Their belief in themselves as such a people is not readily separable from their understanding of the Court invested with the authority to decide their constitutional cases and speak before all others for their constitutional ideals. If the Court's legitimacy should be undermined, then, so would the country be in its very ability to see itself through its constitutional ideals. The Court's concern with legitimacy is not for the sake of the Court, but for the sake of the Nation to which it is responsible.

...A decision to overrule Roe's essential holding under the existing circumstances would address error, if error there was, at the cost of both profound and unnecessary damage to the Court's legitimacy, and to the Nation's commitment to the rule of law. It is therefore imperative to adhere to the essence of Roe's original decision, and we do so today.

Domestic Violence, Pregnancies, and Abortions
(From the Majority Opinion of
Planned Parenthood v. Casey)

...Pennsylvania's abortion law provides, except in cases of medical emergency, that no physician shall perform an abortion on a married woman without receiving a signed statement from the woman that she has notified her spouse that she is about to undergo an abortion...The District Court...made detailed findings of fact regarding the effect of this statute. These included:

"The 'bodily injury' exception could not be invoked by a married woman whose husband, if notified, would, in her reasonable belief, threaten to (a) publicize her intent to have an abortion to family, friends or acquaintances; (b) retaliate against her in future child custody or divorce proceedings; (c) inflict psychological intimidation or emotional harm upon her, her children or other persons; (d) inflict bodily harm on other persons such as children, family members or other loved ones; or (e) use his control over finances to deprive of necessary monies for herself or her children...

"Studies reveal that family violence occurs in two million families in the United States. This figure, however, is a conservative one that substantially understates (because battering is usually not reported until it reaches life-threatening proportions) the actual number of families affected by domestic violence…

"A wife may not elect to notify her husband of her intention to have an abortion for a variety of reasons, including the husband's illness, concern about her own health, the imminent failure of the marriage, or the husband's absolute opposition to the abortion. . .

"Women of all class levels, educational backgrounds, and racial, ethnic and religious groups are battered. . .

"Mere notification of pregnancy is frequently a flashpoint for battering and violence within the family. The number of battering incidents is high during the pregnancy, and often the worst abuse can be associated with pregnancy…The battering husband may deny parentage and use the pregnancy as an excuse for abuse…

"A woman in a shelter or a safe house unknown to her husband is not 'reasonably likely' to have bodily harm inflicted upon her by her batterer; however, her attempt to notify her husband could accidentally disclose her whereabouts to her husband. Her fear of future ramifications would be realistic under the circumstances…

"Because of the nature of the battering relationship, battered women are unlikely to avail themselves of the exceptions to [this] section of the Act, regardless of whether the section applies to them.

These findings are supported by studies of domestic violence. The American Medical Association (AMA) has published a summary of the recent research in this field, which indicates that, in an average 12-month period in this country, approximately two million women are the victims of severe assaults by their male partners. In a 1985 survey, women reported that nearly one of every eight husbands had assaulted their wives during the past year...

The vast majority of women notify their male partners of their decision to obtain an abortion. In many cases in which married women do not notify their husbands, the pregnancy is the result of an extramarital affair. Where the husband is the father, the primary reason women do not notify their husbands is that the husband and wife are experiencing marital difficulties, often accompanied by incidents of violence.[23]

This information and the District Court's findings reinforce what common sense would suggest. In well-functioning marriages, spouses discuss important intimate decisions such as whether to bear a child. But there are millions of women in this country who are the victims of regular physical

---

[23] Ryan & Plutzer, *When Married Women Have Abortions: Spousal Notification and Marital Interaction*, J. Marriage & the Family (1989)

and psychological abuse at the hands of their husbands...

The spousal notification requirement is thus likely to prevent a significant number of women from obtaining an abortion. It does not merely make abortions a little more difficult or expensive to obtain; for many women, it will impose a substantial obstacle...

The unfortunate yet persisting conditions we document above will mean that, in a large fraction of the cases in which [this requirement] is relevant, it will operate as a substantial obstacle to a woman's choice to undergo an abortion. It is an undue burden, and therefore invalid.

This conclusion is in no way inconsistent with our decisions upholding parental notification or consent requirements. Those enactments, and our judgment that they are constitutional, are based on the quite reasonable assumption that minors will benefit from consultation with their parents and that children will often not realize that their parents have their best interests at heart. We cannot adopt a parallel assumption about adult women.

We recognize that a husband has a deep and proper concern and interest...in his wife's pregnancy and in the growth and development of the fetus she is carrying.[24] With regard to the children he has

---

[24] *Planned Parenthood of Central Mo. v. Danforth* (1976)

fathered and raised, the Court has recognized his "cognizable and substantial" interest in their custody. If this case concerned a State's ability to require the mother to notify the father before taking some action with respect to a living child raised by both, therefore, it would be reasonable to conclude, as a general matter, that the father's interest in the welfare of the child and the mother's interest are equal.

Before birth, however, the issue takes on a very different cast. It is an inescapable biological fact that state regulation with respect to the child a woman is carrying will have a far greater impact on the mother's liberty than on the father's... The Court has held that, when the wife and the husband disagree on this decision, the view of only one of the two marriage partners can prevail. Inasmuch as it is the woman who physically bears the child and who is the more directly and immediately affected by the pregnancy, as between the two, the balance weighs in her favor. This conclusion rests upon the basic nature of marriage and the nature of our Constitution: ...The Constitution protects individuals, men and women alike, from unjustified state interference, even when that interference is enacted into law for the benefit of their spouses...

The husband's interest in the life of the child his wife is carrying does not permit the State to empower him with this troubling degree of authority over his wife...If a husband's interest in the potential life of the child outweighs a wife's liberty, the State could require a married woman to notify her husband before she uses a post-fertilization contraceptive. Perhaps next in line would be a statute requiring pregnant married women to notify their husbands before engaging in conduct causing risks to the fetus. After all, if the husband's interest in the fetus' safety is a sufficient predicate for state regulation, the State could reasonably conclude that pregnant wives should notify their husbands before drinking alcohol or smoking. Perhaps married women should notify their husbands before using contraceptives or before undergoing any type of surgery that may have complications affecting the husband's interest in his wife's reproductive organs…A State may not give to a man the kind of dominion over his wife that parents exercise over their children.

[This] Section embodies a view of marriage consonant with the common law status of married women, but repugnant to our present understanding of marriage and of the nature of the rights secured by the Constitution. Women do not lose their constitutionally protected liberty when they marry. The Constitution protects all individuals, male or female, married or unmarried, from the abuse of governmental power, even where that power is employed for the supposed benefit of a member of the individual's family. These considerations confirm our conclusion that [this section] is invalid.

From the Majority Opinion of *Planned Parenthood v. Casey*
(A Divided Majority – with O'Connor, Kennedy, and Souter Joined in Part by Blackmun and Stevens)

[We conclude] that...principles of institutional integrity... require that Roe's essential holding be retained and reaffirmed as to each of its three parts:

(1) a recognition of a woman's right to choose to have an abortion before fetal viability and to obtain it without undue interference from the State...

(2) a confirmation of the State's power to restrict abortions after viability, if the law contains exceptions for pregnancies endangering a woman's life or health

(3) the principle that the State has legitimate interests from the outset of the pregnancy in protecting the health of the woman and the life of the fetus that may become a child.

(a) A reexamination of the principles that define the woman's rights and the State's authority regarding abortions is required by the doubt this Court's subsequent decisions have cast upon the meaning and reach of Roe's central holding, by the fact that the Chief Justice would overrule Roe, and by the necessity that state and federal courts and legislatures have adequate guidance on the subject.

(b) **Roe determined that a woman's decision to terminate her pregnancy is a "liberty" protected against state interference by the substantive component of the Due Process Clause of the Fourteenth Amendment. Neither the Bill of Rights nor the specific practices of States at the time of the Fourteenth Amendment's adoption marks the outer limits of the substantive sphere of such "liberty."** Rather [it] may require this Court to exercise its reasoned judgment in determining the boundaries between the individual's liberty and the demands of organized society...

(d) Although Roe has engendered opposition, it has in no sense proven unworkable, representing as it does a simple limitation beyond which a state law is unenforceable.

(e) **The Roe rule's limitation on state power could not be repudiated without serious inequity to people who, for two decades of economic and social developments, have organized intimate relationships and made choices that define their views of themselves and their places in society, in reliance on the availability of abortion in the event that contraception should fail. The ability of women to participate equally in the economic and social life of the Nation has been facilitated by their ability to control their reproductive lives. The Constitution serves human values, and while the effect of reliance on Roe cannot be** exactly measured, neither can the certain costs of overruling **Roe** for people who have ordered their thinking and living around that case be dismissed...

(g) ...[V]iability marks the earliest point at which the State's interest in fetal life is constitutionally adequate to justify a legislative ban on nontherapeutic abortions. The soundness or unsoundness of that constitutional judgment in no sense turns on when viability occurs...

(i) ...**Only the most convincing justification under accepted standards of precedent could suffice to demonstrate that a later decision overruling the first was anything but a surrender to political pressure and an unjustified repudiation of the principle on which the Court staked its authority in the first instance. Moreover, the country's loss of confidence in the Judiciary would be underscored by condemnation for the Court's failure to keep faith with those who support the decision at a cost to themselves...**

A number of guiding principles [are revealed] that should control the assessment of the Pennsylvania statute:

(a) ...[T]he undue burden standard should be employed. **An undue burden exists, and therefore a provision of law is invalid, if its purpose or effect is to place substantial obstacles in the path** of a woman seeking an abortion before the fetus attains viability.

(b) Roe's rigid trimester framework is rejected. To promote the State's interest in potential life throughout pregnancy, the State may take measures to ensure that the woman's choice is informed. Measures designed to advance this interest should not be invalidated if their purpose is to persuade the woman to choose childbirth over abortion...

(c) As with any medical procedure, the State may enact regulations to further the health or safety of a woman seeking an abortion, but may not impose unnecessary health regulations that present a substantial obstacle to a woman seeking an abortion.

(d) [A] State may not prohibit any woman from making the ultimate decision to terminate her pregnancy before viability.

(e) Roe's holding that "subsequent to viability, the State, in promoting its interest in the potentiality of human life, may, if it chooses, regulate, and even proscribe, abortion except where it is necessary, in appropriate medical judgment, for the preservation of the life or health of the mother" is also reaffirmed.

...[A]ll of the statute's recordkeeping and reporting requirements, except that relating to spousal notice, are constitutional. The reporting provision relating to the reasons a married woman has not notified her husband that she intends to have an abortion must be invalidated, because it places an undue burden on a woman's choice.

…**Requiring that the woman be informed of the availability of information relating to the consequences to the fetus does not interfere with a constitutional right of privacy between a pregnant woman and her physician…Moreover, the physician's First Amendment rights not to speak are implicated only as part of the practice of medicine, which is licensed and regulated by the State…Although [the] 24-hour waiting period may make some abortions more expensive and less convenient, it cannot be said that it is invalid on the present record…**

Section 3206's one-parent consent requirement and judicial bypass procedure are constitutional.[25]

---

[25] See, e.g., *Ohio v. Akron Center for Reproductive Health*

Justice Stevens, Concurring in Part
And Dissenting in Part in
Planned Parenthood v. Casey

...[A]n abortion is not "the termination of life entitled to Fourteenth Amendment protection."...[N]o Member of the Court has ever questioned this fundamental proposition. Thus, as a matter of federal constitutional law, a developing organism that is not yet a "person" does not have what is sometimes described as a "right to life." This has been and, by the Court's holding today, remains, a fundamental premise of our constitutional law governing reproductive autonomy.

...In counterpoise is the woman's constitutional interest in liberty. One aspect of this liberty is a right to bodily integrity, a right to control one's person. This right is neutral on the question of abortion: the Constitution would be equally offended by an absolute requirement that all women undergo abortions as by an absolute prohibition on abortions. "Our whole constitutional heritage rebels at the thought of giving government the power to control men's minds."[26] The same holds true for the power to control women's bodies...

Part of the constitutional liberty to choose is the equal dignity to which each of us is entitled. A woman who decides to terminate her pregnancy is

---

[26] *Stanley v. Georgia* (1969)

entitled to the same respect as a woman who decides to carry the fetus to term. The mandatory waiting period denies women that equal respect...

The 24-hour delay requirement fails both parts of this test. The findings of the District Court establish the severity of the burden that the 24-hour delay imposes on many pregnant women. Yet even in those cases in which the delay is not especially onerous, it is, in my opinion, "undue," because there is no evidence that such a delay serves a useful and legitimate purpose. As indicated above, there is no legitimate reason to require a woman who has agonized over her decision to leave the clinic or hospital and return again another day...[A] rigid requirement that all patients wait 24 hours or (what is true in practice) much longer to evaluate the significance of information that is either common knowledge or irrelevant is an irrational, and therefore "undue," burden.

The counseling provisions are similarly infirm...I conclude that the information requirements do not serve a useful purpose, and thus constitute an unnecessary - and therefore undue - burden on the woman's constitutional liberty to decide to terminate her pregnancy.

Accordingly, while I disagree with Parts IV, V-B, and V-D of the joint opinion, I join the remainder of the Court's opinion.

Justice Blackmun, Concurring in Part, Concurring in the Judgment in Part, And Dissenting in Part

Three years ago,[27] four Members of this Court appeared poised to "cas[t] into darkness the hopes and visions of every woman in this country" who had come to believe that the Constitution guaranteed her the right to reproductive choice.[28] All that remained between the promise of Roe and the darkness of the plurality was a single, flickering flame. Decisions since Webster[29] gave little reason to hope that this flame would cast much light. But now, just when so many expected the darkness to fall, the flame has grown bright.

...I remain steadfast in my belief that the right to reproductive choice is entitled to the full protection afforded by this Court before Webster. And I fear for the darkness as four Justices anxiously await the single vote necessary to extinguish the light...

Today a majority reaffirms that the Due Process Clause of the Fourteenth Amendment establishes "a realm of personal liberty which the government may not enter"...Further, when the

---

[27] In *Webster v. Reproductive Health Services* (1989)
[28] Blackmun, J., dissenting
[29] *Webster v. Reproductive Health Services*

State restricts a woman's right to terminate her pregnancy, it deprives a woman of the right to make her own decision about reproduction and family planning - critical life choices that this Court long has deemed central to the right to privacy...Because motherhood has a dramatic impact on a woman's educational prospects, employment opportunities, and self-determination, restrictive abortion laws deprive her of basic control over her life...

A State's restrictions on a woman's right to terminate her pregnancy also implicate constitutional guarantees of gender equality. State restrictions on abortion compel women to continue pregnancies they otherwise might terminate. By restricting the right to terminate pregnancies, the State conscripts women's bodies into its service, forcing women to continue their pregnancies, suffer the pains of childbirth, and in most instances, provide years of maternal care. The State does not compensate women for their services; instead, it assumes that they owe this duty as a matter of course. This assumption - that women can simply be forced to accept the "natural" status and incidents of motherhood - appears to rest upon a conception of women's role that has triggered the protection of the Equal Protection Clause...The joint opinion recognizes that these assumptions about women's place in society "are no longer consistent with our understanding of the family, the individual, or the Constitution."

...[T]he trimester framework is attacked because its key elements do not appear in the text of the Constitution. My response to this attack remains the same as it was in Webster: "Were this a true concern, we would have to abandon most of our constitutional jurisprudence. [T]he "critical elements" of countless constitutional doctrines nowhere appear in the Constitution's text. . .The Constitution makes no mention, for example, of the First Amendment's "actual malice" standard for proving certain libels[30]...Similarly, the Constitution makes no mention of the rational basis test, or the specific verbal formulations of intermediate and strict scrutiny by which this Court evaluates claims under the Equal Protection Clause. The reason is simple. Like the Roe framework, these tests or standards are not, and do not purport to be, rights protected by the Constitution. Rather, they are judge-made methods for evaluating and measuring the strength and scope of constitutional rights or for balancing the constitutional rights of individuals against the competing interests of government.

The second criticism is that the framework more closely resembles a regulatory code than a body of constitutional doctrine. Again, my answer remains the same as in Webster: "[I]f this were a true and genuine concern, we would have to abandon vast areas of our constitutional jurisprudence...Are [the

---

[30] See *New York Times Co. v. Sullivan* (1964)

distinctions entailed in the trimester framework] any finer, or more "regulatory," than the distinctions we have often drawn in our First Amendment jurisprudence, where, for example, we have held that a "release time" program permitting public school students to leave school grounds during school hours to receive religious instruction does not violate the Establishment Clause, even though a release time program permitting religious instruction on school grounds does violate the Clause?

...Again, I stand by the views I expressed in Webster: "I remain convinced, as six other Members of this Court 16 years ago were convinced, that the Roe framework, and the viability standard in particular, fairly, sensibly, and effectively functions to safeguard the constitutional liberties of pregnant women while recognizing and accommodating the State's interest in potential human life.

...In sum, I would affirm the judgment in No. 91-902 and reverse the judgment in No. 91-744...I am 83 years old. I cannot remain on this Court forever, and when I do step down, the confirmation process for my successor well may focus on the issue before us today. That, I regret, may be exactly where the choice between the two worlds will be made.

Minority Opinion in *Planned Parenthood* by the Chief Justice
(Joined by Justice White, Justice Scalia, and Justice Thomas)

Although *Roe v. Wade*, is not directly implicated by the Pennsylvania statute, which simply regulates, and does not prohibit, abortion, a reexamination of the "fundamental right" Roe accorded to a woman's decision to abort a fetus, with the concomitant requirement that any state regulation of abortion survive "strict scrutiny," is warranted by the confusing and uncertain state of this Court's post-Roe decisional law. A review of post-Roe cases demonstrates both that they have expanded upon Roe in imposing increasingly greater restrictions on the States,[31] and that the Court has become increasingly more divided, none of the last three such decisions having commanded a majority opinion.[32]

The Roe Court reached too far when it analogized the right to abort a fetus to the rights involved in *Pierce v. Society of Sisters; Meyer v. Nebraska; Loving v. Virginia;* and *Griswold v. Connecticut,* and thereby deemed the right to abortion to be

---

[31] See *Thornburgh v. American College of Obstetricians and Gynecologists*

[32] See *Ohio v. Akron Center for Reproductive Health; Hodgson v. Minnesota; Webster v. Reproductive Health Services*

"fundamental." None of these decisions endorsed an all-encompassing "right of privacy," as *Roe* claimed. Because abortion involves the purposeful termination of potential life, the abortion decision must be recognized as…different in kind from the rights protected in the earlier cases…**And the historical traditions of the American people - as evidenced by the English common law and by the American abortion statutes in existence both at the time of the Fourteenth Amendment's adoption and Roe's issuance - do not support the view that the right to terminate one's pregnancy is "fundamental." Thus, enactments abridging that right need not be subjected to strict scrutiny.**

The undue burden standard adopted by the joint [Majority] opinion …has no basis in constitutional law, and will not result in the sort of simple limitation, easily applied, which the opinion anticipates. To evaluate abortion regulations under that standard, judges will have to make the subjective, unguided determination whether the regulations place "substantial obstacles" in the path of a woman seeking an abortion, undoubtedly engendering a variety of conflicting views. **The standard presents nothing more workable than the trimester framework the joint opinion discards, and will allow the Court, under the guise of the Constitution, to continue to impart** its own preferences on the States in the form of a complex abortion code.

The correct analysis is that set forth by the plurality opinion in Webster: a woman's interest in having an abortion is a form of liberty protected by the Due Process Clause, but States may regulate abortion procedures in ways rationally related to a legitimate state interest.

...The requirement that a physician disclose certain information about the abortion procedure and its risks and alternatives is not a large burden, and is clearly related to maternal health and the State's interest in informed consent...That such information might create some uncertainty and persuade some women to forgo abortions only demonstrates that it might make a difference, and is therefore relevant to a woman's informed choice...For the same reason, this Court's previous holding invalidating a State's 24-hour mandatory waiting period should not be followed. The waiting period helps ensure that a woman's decision to abort is a well-considered one, and rationally furthers the State's legitimate interest in maternal health and in unborn life. It may delay, but does not prohibit, abortions; and both it and the informed consent provisions do not apply in medical emergencies...

Chief Justice Rehnquist, with whom Justice White, Justice Scalia, and Justice Thomas Join, Concurring in the Judgment in Part and Dissenting in Part in *Planned Parenthood v. Casey*

The joint opinion...retains the outer shell of *Roe v. Wade* (1973), but beats a wholesale retreat from the substance of that case. We believe that Roe was wrongly decided, and that it can and should be overruled consistently...We would adopt the approach of the plurality in *Webster v. Reproductive Health Services* (1989), and uphold the challenged provisions of the Pennsylvania statute in their entirety...

We have not allowed States much leeway to regulate even the actual abortion procedure...In *Colautti v. Franklin* (1979), the Court struck down a statute that governed the determination of viability. In the process, we made clear that the trimester framework incorporated only one definition of viability - ours - as we forbade States from deciding that a certain objective indicator - "be it weeks of gestation or fetal weight or any other single factor" - should govern the definition of viability. In that same case, we also invalidated a regulation requiring a physician to use the abortion technique offering the best chance for fetal survival when performing postviability abortions. In *Thornburgh v. American*

College of Obstetricians and Gynecologists, the Court struck down Pennsylvania's requirement that a second physician be present at postviability abortions to help preserve the health of the unborn child, on the ground that it did not incorporate a sufficient medical emergency exception. Regulations governing the treatment of aborted fetuses have met a similar fate. In Akron, we invalidated a provision requiring physicians performing abortions to "insure that the remains of the unborn child are disposed of in a humane and sanitary manner."

Dissents in these cases expressed the view that the Court was expanding upon Roe in imposing ever greater restrictions on the States.[33] And, when confronted with State regulations of this type in past years, the Court has become increasingly more divided: The three most recent abortion cases have not commanded a Court opinion.[34]

…In *Roe v. Wade*, the Court recognized a "guarantee of personal privacy" which "is broad enough to encompass a woman's decision whether or not to terminate her pregnancy." [But] unlike marriage, procreation, and contraception, abortion "involves the purposeful termination of a potential

---

[33] Including *Thornburgh v. American College of Obstetricians*
[34] *Ohio v. Akron Center; Hodgson v. Minnesota; Webster v. Reproductive Health Services*

life."[35] ... (To look "at the act which is assertedly the subject of a liberty interest in isolation from its effect upon other people [is] like inquiring whether there is a liberty interest in firing a gun where the case at hand happens to involve its discharge into another person's body.")

Nor do the historical traditions of the American people support the view that the right to terminate one's pregnancy is "fundamental." The common law which we inherited from England made abortion after "quickening" an offense. At the time of the adoption of the Fourteenth Amendment, statutory prohibitions or restrictions on abortion were commonplace; in 1868, at least 28 of the then-37 States and 8 Territories had statutes banning or limiting abortion.[36] By the turn of the century, virtually every State had a law prohibiting or restricting abortion on its books. By the middle of the present century, a liberalization trend had set in. But 21 of the restrictive abortion laws in effect in 1868 were still in effect in 1973 when Roe was decided, and an overwhelming majority of the States prohibited abortion unless necessary to preserve the life or health of the mother.[37] On this record, it can scarcely be said that any deeply rooted tradition of relatively unrestricted abortion in our

---

[35] *Harris v. McRae* (1980)

[36] J. Mohr, *Abortion in America* (1978)

[37] *Roe v. Wade* (Rehnquist, J., dissenting)

history supported the classification of the right to abortion as "fundamental" under the Due Process Clause of the Fourteenth Amendment.

We think, therefore, both in view of this history and of our decided cases dealing with substantive liberty under the Due Process Clause, that the Court was mistaken in Roe when it classified a woman's decision to terminate her pregnancy as a "fundamental right" that could be abridged only in a manner which withstood "strict scrutiny."

…We believe that the sort of constitutionally imposed abortion code of the type illustrated by our decisions following Roe is inconsistent "with the notion of a Constitution cast in general terms, as ours is, and usually speaking in general principles, as ours does."[38]…

Our constitutional watch does not cease merely because we have spoken before on an issue; when it becomes clear that a prior constitutional interpretation is unsound, we are obliged to reexamine the question.

The joint opinion discusses several…factors which, it asserts, point toward retaining a portion of Roe. Two of these factors are that the main "factual underpinning" of Roe has remained the same, and that its doctrinal foundation is no weaker now than it was in 1973. Of course, what might be called the

---

[38] *Webster v. Reproductive Health Services* (plurality opinion)

basic facts which gave rise to Roe have remained the same - women become pregnant, there is a point somewhere, depending on medical technology, where a fetus becomes viable, and women give birth to children. But this is only to say that the same facts which gave rise to Roe will continue to give rise to similar cases...And surely there is no requirement...that a decision be more wrong now than it was at the time it was rendered. If that were true, the most outlandish constitutional decision could survive forever, based simply on the fact that it was no more outlandish later than it was when originally rendered...

Under this principle, when the Court has ruled on a divisive issue, it is apparently prevented from overruling that decision for the sole reason that it was incorrect, unless opposition to the original decision has died away.

The first difficulty with this principle lies in its assumption that cases that are "intensely divisive" can be readily distinguished from those that are not...In addition, because the Court's duty is to ignore public opinion and criticism on issues that come before it, its Members are in perhaps the worst position to judge whether a decision divides the Nation deeply enough to justify such uncommon protection. **Although many of the Court's decisions divide the populace to a large degree, we have not previously on that account shied away...when urged to reconsider earlier**

106

decisions. Over the past 21 years, for example, the Court has overruled in whole or in part 34 of its previous constitutional decisions...

There are other reasons why the joint opinion's discussion of legitimacy is unconvincing, as well. **In assuming that the Court is perceived as "surrender[ing] to political pressure" when it overrules a controversial decision, the joint opinion forgets that there are two sides to any controversy.** The joint opinion asserts that, in order to protect its legitimacy, the Court must refrain from overruling a controversial decision lest it be viewed as favoring those who oppose the decision. But a decision to adhere to prior precedent is subject to the same criticism, for, in such a case, one can easily argue that the Court is responding to those who have demonstrated in favor of the original decision. The decision in Roe has engendered large demonstrations, including repeated marches on this Court and on Congress, both in opposition to and in support of that opinion. A decision either way on Roe can therefore be perceived as favoring one group or the other. But this perceived dilemma arises only if one assumes, as the joint opinion does, that the Court should make its decisions with a view toward speculative public perceptions. **If one assumes instead, as the Court surely did in both Brown and West Coast Hotel, that the Court's legitimacy is enhanced by faithful interpretation of the Constitution**

irrespective of public opposition, such self-engendered difficulties may be put to one side.

Roe is not this Court's only decision to generate conflict. Our decisions in some recent capital cases, and in *Bowers v. Hardwick* have also engendered demonstrations in opposition. The joint opinion's message to such protesters appears to be that they must cease their activities in order to serve their cause, because their protests will only cement in place a decision which, by normal standards...should be reconsidered. Nearly a century ago, Justice David J. Brewer of this Court, in an article discussing criticism of its decisions, observed that "many criticisms may be, like their authors, devoid of good taste, but better all sorts of criticism than no criticism at all."[39] **This was good advice to the Court then, as it is today. Strong and often misguided criticism of a decision should not render the decision immune from reconsideration, lest a fetish for legitimacy penalize freedom of expression.**

The end result of the joint opinion's paeans of praise for legitimacy is the enunciation of a brand new standard for evaluating state regulation of a woman's right to abortion - the "undue burden" standard. As indicated above, *Roe v. Wade* adopted a "fundamental right" standard under which state regulations could survive only if they met the

---

[39] Justice Brewer on "The Nation's Anchor" (1898)

requirement of "strict scrutiny." While we disagree with that standard, it at least had a recognized basis in constitutional law at the time Roe was decided. The same cannot be said for the "undue burden" standard, which is created largely out of whole cloth by the authors of the joint opinion. It is a standard which even today does not command the support of a majority of this Court. And it will not, we believe, result in the sort of "simple limitation," easily applied, which the joint opinion anticipates. In sum, it is a standard which is not built to last.

In evaluating abortion regulations under that standard, judges will have to decide whether they place a "substantial obstacle" in the path of a woman seeking an abortion. In that this standard is based even more on a judge's subjective determinations than was the trimester framework, the standard will do nothing to prevent "judges from roaming at large in the constitutional field," guided only by their personal views.[40] Because the undue burden standard is plucked from nowhere, the question of what is a "substantial obstacle" to abortion will undoubtedly engender a variety of conflicting views. For example, in the very matter before us now, the authors of the joint opinion would uphold Pennsylvania's 24-hour waiting period, concluding that a "particular burden" on some women is not a substantial obstacle. But the

---

[40] *Griswold v. Connecticut* (Harlan, J., concurring in judgment)

authors would at the same time strike down Pennsylvania's spousal notice provision, after finding that, in a "large fraction" of cases, the provision will be a substantial obstacle. And, while the authors conclude that the informed consent provisions do not constitute an "undue burden," Justice Stevens would hold that they do.

...Accordingly, we think that the correct analysis is that set forth by the plurality opinion in Webster. A woman's interest in having an abortion is a form of liberty protected by the Due Process Clause, but States may regulate abortion procedures in ways rationally related to a legitimate state interest.[41] With this rule in mind, we examine each of the challenged provisions.

...Section 3205(a)(2) compels the disclosure, by a physician or a counselor, of information concerning the availability of paternal child support and state-funded alternatives if the woman decides to proceed with her pregnancy...That the information might create some uncertainty and persuade some women to forgo abortions does not lead to the conclusion that the Constitution forbids the provision of such information. Indeed, it only demonstrates that this information might very well make a difference, and that it is therefore relevant to

---

[41] *Williamson v. Lee Optical of Oklahoma, Inc.* (1955); *Stanley v. Illinois* (1972)

a woman's informed choice. **White, J., dissenting, wrote: "[T]he ostensible objective of *Roe v. Wade* is not maximizing the number of abortions, but maximizing choice."**

...Section 3209 of the Act contains the spousal notification provision...We first emphasize that Pennsylvania has not imposed a spousal consent requirement of the type the Court struck down in *Planned Parenthood of Central Mo. v. Danforth.* Missouri's spousal consent provision was invalidated in that case because of the Court's view that it unconstitutionally granted to the husband "a veto power exercisable for any reason whatsoever or for no reason at all." But the provision here involves a much less intrusive requirement of spousal notification, not consent...

The question before us is therefore whether the spousal notification requirement rationally furthers any legitimate state interests. We conclude that it does...As Judge Alito observed in his dissent below, [t]he Pennsylvania legislature could have rationally believed that some married women are initially inclined to obtain an abortion without their husbands' knowledge because of perceived problems - such as economic constraints, future plans, or the husbands' previously expressed opposition - that may be obviated by discussion prior to the abortion.

The State also has a legitimate interest in promoting "the integrity of the marital relationship."

This Court has previously recognized "the importance of the marital relationship in our society."[42] In our view, the spousal notice requirement is a rational attempt by the State to improve truthful communication between spouses and encourage collaborative decisionmaking, and thereby fosters marital integrity.[43]... We therefore conclude that the spousal notice provision comports with the Constitution.[44]

...For the reasons stated, we therefore would hold that each of the challenged provisions of the Pennsylvania statute is consistent with the Constitution. It bears emphasis that our conclusion in this regard does not carry with it any necessary approval of these regulations. Our task is, as always, to decide only whether the challenged provisions of a law comport with the United States Constitution. If, as we believe, these do, their wisdom as a matter of public policy is for the people of Pennsylvania to decide.

---

[42] *Planned Parenthood of Central Mo. v. Danforth*

[43] See *Labine v. Vincent* (1971)

[44] See *Harris v. McRae* ("It is not the mission of this Court or any other to decide whether the balance of competing interests . . . is wise social policy.")

Justice Scalia, with Whom the Chief Justice, Justice White, and Justice Thomas Join, Concurring in the Judgment in Part and Dissenting in Part

My views on this matter are unchanged from those I set forth in my separate opinions in *Webster v. Reproductive Health Services* (1989).[45] **The States may, if they wish, permit abortion on demand, but the Constitution does not require them to do so. The permissibility of abortion, and the limitations upon it, are to be resolved like most important questions in our democracy: by citizens trying to persuade one another and then voting. As the Court acknowledges, "where reasonable people disagree, the government can adopt one position or the other." ...A State's choice between two positions on which reasonable people can disagree is constitutional even when (as is often the case) it intrudes upon a "liberty" in the absolute sense.** Laws against bigamy, for example - with which entire societies of reasonable people disagree - intrude upon men and women's liberty to marry and live with one another. But bigamy happens not to be a liberty specially "protected" by the Constitution.

---

[45] And *Ohio v. Akron Center for Reproductive Health*

113

That is, quite simply, the issue in this case: not whether the power of a woman to abort her unborn child is a "liberty" in the absolute sense; or even whether it is a liberty of great importance to many women. Of course it is both. The issue is whether it is a liberty protected by the Constitution of the United States. I am sure it is not. I reach that conclusion not because of anything so exalted as my views concerning the "concept of existence, of meaning, of the universe, and of the mystery of human life." Rather, I reach it for the same reason I reach the conclusion that bigamy is not constitutionally protected - because of two simple facts: (1) the Constitution says absolutely nothing about it, and (2) the longstanding traditions of American society have permitted it to be legally proscribed.[46]

...Beyond that brief summary of the essence of my position, I will not swell the United States Reports with repetition of what I have said before; and applying the rational basis test, I would uphold the Pennsylvania statute in its entirety. I must, however, respond to a few of the more outrageous arguments in today's opinion, which it is beyond human nature to leave unanswered...

Today's opinion describes the methodology of Roe, quite accurately, as weighing against the woman's interest the State's "'important and

---

[46] Akron II (Scalia, J., concurring)

legitimate interest in protecting the potentiality of human life.'" But "reasoned judgment" does not begin by...assuming that what the State is protecting is the mere "potentiality of human life." **The whole argument of abortion opponents is that what the Court calls the fetus and what others call the unborn child is a human life. Thus, whatever answer Roe came up with after conducting its "balancing" is bound to be wrong, unless it is correct that the human fetus is in some critical sense merely potentially human. There is, of course, no way to determine that as a legal matter; it is, in fact, a value judgment. Some societies have considered newborn children not yet human, or the incompetent elderly no longer so.**

...The emptiness of the "reasoned judgment" that produced Roe is displayed in plain view by the fact that, after more than 19 years of effort by some of the brightest (and most determined) legal minds in the country, after more than 10 cases upholding abortion rights in this Court...the best the Court can do to explain how it is that the word "liberty" must be thought to include the right to destroy human fetuses is to rattle off a collection of adjectives that simply decorate a value judgment and conceal a political choice. The right to abort, we are told, inheres in "liberty" because it is among "a person's most basic decisions," it involves a "most intimate and personal choic[e]," it is "central to personal dignity and autonomy,"; it "originate[s]" within the zone of conscience and belief," it is "too intimate and personal" for state interference, it reflects "intimate views" of a "deep, personal character," it involves "intimate relationships" and notions of "personal autonomy and bodily integrity," and it concerns a particularly "`important decisio[n],'" But it is obvious to anyone applying "reasoned judgment" that the same adjectives can be applied to many forms of conduct that this Court[47] has held are not entitled to constitutional protection - because, like abortion, they are forms of conduct that have long been criminalized in American society...It is not reasoned judgment that supports the Court's decision; only personal predilection.

Justice Curtis' warning is as timely today as it was 135 years ago: "[W]hen a strict interpretation of the Constitution, according to the fixed rules which govern the interpretation of laws, is abandoned, and the theoretical opinions of individuals are allowed to control its meaning, we have no longer a Constitution; we are under the government of individual men, who for the time being have power to declare what the Constitution is, according to their own views of what it ought to mean."[48]

---

[47] See *Bowers v. Hardwick* (1986)
[48] *Dred Scott v. Sandford* (dissenting opinion)

...The shortcomings of Roe did not include lack of clarity: virtually all regulation of abortion before the third trimester was invalid. But to come across this phrase in the joint opinion - which calls upon federal district judges to apply an "undue burden" standard as doubtful in application as it is unprincipled in origin - is really more than one should have to bear.

...Justice O'Connor has also abandoned (again without explanation) the view she expressed in *Planned Parenthood Assn. of Kansas City, Mo., Inc. v. Ashcroft* that a medical regulation which imposes an "undue burden" could nevertheless be upheld if it "reasonably relate[s] to the preservation and protection of maternal health." In today's version, even health measures will be upheld only "if they do not constitute an undue burden." Gone too is Justice O'Connor's statement that "the State possesses compelling interests in the protection of potential human life...throughout pregnancy,"[49] instead, the State's interest in unborn human life is stealthily downgraded to a merely "substantial" or "profound" interest. That had to be done, of course, since designating the interest as "compelling" throughout pregnancy would have been, shall we say, a "substantial obstacle" to the joint opinion's determined effort to reaffirm what it views as the "central holding" of Roe...It is difficult to maintain

---

[49] Akron I (dissenting opinion)

the illusion that we are interpreting a Constitution, rather than inventing one, when we amend its provisions so breezily...

I am certainly not in a good position to dispute that the Court has saved the "central holding" of Roe, since, to do that effectively, I would have to know what the Court has saved, which in turn would require me to understand (as I do not) what the "undue burden" test means. I must confess, however, that I have always thought, and I think a lot of other people have always thought, that the arbitrary trimester framework, which the Court today discards, was quite as central to Roe as the arbitrary viability test, which the Court today retains. It seems particularly ungrateful to carve the trimester framework out of the core of Roe, since its very rigidity (in sharp contrast to the utter indeterminability of the "undue burden" test) is probably the only reason the Court is able to say...that Roe "has in no sense proven 'unworkable.'" I suppose the Court is entitled to call a "central holding" whatever it wants to call a "central holding."...I thought I might note, however, that the following portions of Roe have not been saved:

* Under Roe, requiring that a woman seeking an abortion be provided truthful information about abortion before giving informed written consent is unconstitutional if the information is designed to influence her choice. Under the joint opinion's

"undue burden" regime (as applied today, at least) such a requirement is constitutional...

* Under Roe, requiring a 24-hour waiting period between the time the woman gives her informed consent and the time of the abortion is unconstitutional. Under the "undue burden" regime (as applied today, at least) it is not.

* Under Roe, requiring detailed reports that include demographic data about each woman who seeks an abortion and various information about each abortion is unconstitutional. Under the "undue burden" regime (as applied today, at least) it generally is not...

The Court's description of the place of Roe in the social history of the United States is unrecognizable. Not only did Roe not, as the Court suggests, resolve the deeply divisive issue of abortion; it did more than anything else to nourish it, by elevating it to the national level, where it is infinitely more difficult to resolve. National politics were not plagued by abortion protests, national abortion lobbying, or abortion marches on Congress before *Roe v. Wade* was decided. Profound disagreement existed among our citizens over the issue - as it does over other issues, such as the death penalty - but that disagreement was being worked out at the state level. As with many other issues, the division of sentiment within each State was not as closely balanced as it was among the population of the

Nation as a whole, meaning not only that more people would be satisfied with the results of state-by-state resolution, but also that those results would be more stable. Pre-Roe, moreover, political compromise was possible.

Roe's mandate for abortion on demand destroyed the compromises of the past, rendered compromise impossible for the future, and required the entire issue to be resolved uniformly, at the national level. At the same time, Roe created a vast new class of abortion consumers and abortion proponents by eliminating the moral opprobrium that had attached to the act. ("If the Constitution guarantees abortion, how can it be bad?" - not an accurate line of thought, but a natural one.) Many favor all of those developments, and it is not for me to say that they are wrong. But to portray Roe as the statesmanlike "settlement" of a divisive issue, a jurisprudential Peace of Westphalia that is worth preserving, is nothing less than Orwellian. Roe fanned into life an issue that has inflamed our national politics in general, and has obscured with its smoke the selection of Justices to this Court, in particular, ever since. And by keeping us in the abortion-umpiring business, it is the perpetuation of that disruption, rather than of any Pax Roeana that the Court's new majority decrees...

[From the Majority]: "… If the Court's legitimacy should be undermined, then so would the country be in its very ability to see itself through its constitutional ideals."

The Imperial Judiciary lives. It is instructive to compare this Nietzschean vision of us unelected, life-tenured judges - leading a Volk who will be "tested by following," and whose very "belief in themselves" is mystically bound up in their "understanding" of a Court that "speak[s] before all others for their constitutional ideals" - with the somewhat more modest role envisioned for these lawyers by the Founders.

"The judiciary . . . has . . . no direction either of the strength or of the wealth of the society, and can take no active resolution whatever. It may truly be said to have neither Force nor Will, but merely judgment. . . ." (The Federalist No. 78)

…"[T]he candid citizen must confess that, if the policy of the Government upon vital questions affecting the whole people is to be irrevocably fixed by decisions of the Supreme Court . . . the people will have ceased to be their own rulers, having to that extent practically resigned their Government into the hands of that eminent tribunal." (A. Lincoln, First Inaugural Address, Mar. 4, 1861)

…That is not a principle of law (which is what I thought the Court was talking about), but a principle of Realpolitik - and a wrong one, at that.

I cannot agree with, indeed I am appalled by, the Court's suggestion that the decision whether to stand by an erroneous constitutional decision must be strongly influenced - against overruling, no less - by the substantial and continuing public opposition the decision has generated. The Court's judgment that any other course would "subvert the Court's legitimacy" must be another consequence of reading the error-filled history book that described the deeply divided country brought together by Roe. In my history book, the Court was covered with dishonor and deprived of legitimacy by *Dred Scott v. Sandford* (1857), an erroneous (and widely opposed) opinion that it did not abandon, rather than by *West Coast Hotel Co. v. Parrish* (1937)...Indeed, Dred Scott was very possibly the first application of substantive due process in the Supreme Court...[50]

But whether it would "subvert the Court's legitimacy" or not, the notion that we would decide a case differently from the way we otherwise would have in order to show that we can stand firm against public disapproval is frightening. It is a bad enough idea, even in the head of someone like me, who believes that the text of the Constitution, and our traditions, say what they say and there is no fiddling with them...[T]he notion that the Court must adhere to a decision for as long as the decision faces "great

[50] D. Currie, *The Constitution in the Supreme Court* (1985)

opposition" and the Court is "under fire" acquires a character of almost czarist arrogance. **We are offended by these marchers who descend upon us, every year on the anniversary of Roe, to protest our saying that the Constitution requires what our society has never thought the Constitution requires. These people who refuse to be "tested by following" must be taught a lesson. We have no Cossacks, but at least we can stubbornly refuse to abandon an erroneous opinion that we might otherwise change - to show how little they intimidate us.**

...Instead of engaging in the hopeless task of predicting public perception - a job not for lawyers but for political campaign managers - the Justices should do what is legally right by asking two questions: (1) Was Roe correctly decided? (2) Has Roe succeeded in producing a settled body of law? If the answer to both questions is no, Roe should undoubtedly be overruled.

In truth, I am as distressed as the Court is - and expressed my distress several years ago[51]- about the "political pressure" directed to the Court: the marches, the mail, the protests aimed at inducing us to change our opinions. How upsetting it is, that so many of our citizens (good people, not lawless ones, on both sides of this abortion issue, and on various sides of other issues as well) think that we Justices

---

[51] See *Webster v. Reproductive Health Services* (1989)

should properly take into account their views, as though we were engaged not in ascertaining an objective law, but in determining some kind of social consensus. **The Court would profit, I think, from giving less attention to the fact of this distressing phenomenon, and more attention to the cause of it. That cause permeates today's opinion: a new mode of constitutional adjudication that relies not upon text and traditional practice to determine the law, but upon what the Court calls "reasoned judgment, "which turns out to be nothing but philosophical predilection and moral intuition.** All manner of "liberties," the Court tells us, inhere in the Constitution, and are enforceable by this Court - not just those mentioned in the text or established in the traditions of our society. **Why even the Ninth Amendment - which says only that "[t]he enumeration in the Constitution, of certain rights, shall not be construed to deny or disparage others retained by the people" - is, despite our contrary understanding for almost 200 years, a literally boundless source of additional, unnamed, unhinted-at "rights," definable and enforceable by us, through "reasoned judgment." What makes all this relevant to the bothersome application of "political pressure" against the Court are the twin facts that the American people love democracy and the American people are not fools.** As long as this Court thought (and the people thought) that we Justices were doing essentially lawyers' work up here - reading text and discerning our society's traditional understanding of that text - the public pretty much left us alone. Texts and traditions are facts to study, not convictions to demonstrate about. But if in reality, our process of constitutional adjudication consists primarily of making value judgments; if we can ignore a long and clear tradition clarifying an ambiguous text, as we did, for example, five days ago in declaring unconstitutional invocations and benedictions at public high school graduation ceremonies;[52] if, as I say, our pronouncement of constitutional law rests primarily on value judgments, then a free and intelligent people's attitude towards us can be expected to be (ought to be) quite different. **The people know that their value judgments are quite as good as those taught in any law school - maybe better. If, indeed, the "liberties" protected by the Constitution are, as the Court says, undefined and unbounded, then the people should demonstrate, to protest that we do not implement their values instead of ours.** Not only that, but the confirmation hearings for new Justices should deteriorate into question-and-answer sessions in which Senators go through a list of their constituents' most favored and most disfavored alleged constitutional rights, and seek the nominee's

---

[52] *Lee v. Weisman* (1992)

commitment to support or oppose them. **Value judgments, after all, should be voted on, not dictated; and if our Constitution has somehow accidentally committed them to the Supreme Court, at least we can have a sort of plebiscite each time a new nominee to that body is put forward...**

There is a poignant aspect to today's opinion. Its length, and what might be called its epic tone, suggest that its authors believe they are bringing to an end a troublesome era in the history of our Nation, and of our Court. "It is the dimension" of authority, they say, to cal[l] the contending sides of national controversy to end their national division by accepting a common mandate rooted in the Constitution.

There comes vividly to mind a portrait by Emanuel Leutze that hangs in the Harvard Law School: Roger Brooke Taney, painted in 1859, the 82nd year of his life, the 24th of his Chief Justiceship, the second after his opinion in Dred Scott. He is in black, sitting in a shadowed red armchair, left hand resting upon a pad of paper in his lap, right hand hanging limply, almost lifelessly, beside the inner arm of the chair. He sits facing the viewer and staring straight out. There seems to be on his face, and in his deep-set eyes, an expression of profound sadness and disillusionment. Perhaps he always looked that way, even when dwelling upon the happiest of thoughts. But those of us who know how the lustre of his great Chief Justiceship came to be eclipsed by Dred Scott cannot help believing that he had that case - its already apparent consequences for the Court and its soon-to-be-played-out consequences for the Nation - burning on his mind. I expect that, two years earlier, he, too, had thought himself call[ing] the contending sides of national controversy to end their national division by accepting a common mandate rooted in the Constitution.

It is no more realistic for us in this case than it was for him in that to think that an issue of the sort they both involved - an issue involving life and death, freedom and subjugation - can be "speedily and finally settled" by the Supreme Court, as President James Buchanan, in his inaugural address, said the issue of slavery in the territories would be. **Quite to the contrary, by foreclosing all democratic outlet for the deep passions this issue arouses, by banishing the issue from the political forum that gives all participants, even the losers, the satisfaction of a fair hearing and an honest fight, by continuing the imposition of a rigid national rule instead of allowing for regional differences, the Court merely prolongs and intensifies the anguish.**

We should get out of this area, where we have no right to be, and where we do neither ourselves nor the country any good by remaining.

Conclusion

I read and reread these opinions, alternating between wanting to cry (when I was reading most of the Majority Opinions) and wanting to smile (when I was reading the Opinions by Justices White, Rehnquist, and Scalia).

The fight to rein in abortions in this country has felt like an uphill battle for more than forty years, oftentimes a battle that can't be won. But I see hope in the midst of these words – hope that states have not completely lost the ability to make laws to limit abortions; maybe we've just stopped fighting too soon. It will take a change in the makeup of the current Supreme Court to completely overturn Roe, but in the meantime, it's time to at least reduce the numbers. It is sad to think that more than two generations of women in America have grown up believing they can use abortions as an acceptable method of birth control.

For more information on this important topic, I recommend the website: **EndRoe.org**. I like their position statement: *"The purpose of **EndRoe.org** is to promote a fuller understanding of what the Court did in Roe and Doe and why these fundamentally erroneous decisions must be corrected."* I couldn't agree more! There you will find a great timeline of the Supreme Court cases dealing with abortion, and more information on each of those. I do look forward to the day that we have helped bring an end to Roe!

First, Fourth, Fifth, Ninth, and Fourteenth Amendments

First Amendment:

Congress shall make no law respecting an establishment of religion, or prohibiting the free exercise thereof; or abridging the freedom of speech, or of the press; or the right of the people peaceably to assemble, and to petition the Government for a redress of grievances.

Fourth Amendment:

The right of the people to be secure in their persons, houses, papers, and effects, against unreasonable searches and seizures, shall not be violated, and no Warrants shall issue, but upon probable cause, supported by Oath or affirmation, and particularly describing the place to be searched, and the persons or things to be seized.

Fifth Amendment:

No person shall be held to answer for a capital, or otherwise infamous crime, unless on a presentment or indictment of a Grand Jury, except in cases arising in the land or naval forces, or in the Militia, when in actual service in time of War or public danger; nor shall any person be subject for the same offence to be twice put in jeopardy of life or limb; nor shall be compelled in any criminal case to be a witness against himself, nor be deprived of life, liberty, or property, without due process of law; nor shall private property be taken for public use, without just compensation.

Ninth Amendment:

The enumeration in the Constitution, of certain rights, shall not be construed to deny or disparage others retained by the people.

Fourteenth Amendment, Section 1:

All persons born or naturalized in the United States, and subject to the jurisdiction thereof, are citizens of the United States and of the State wherein they reside. No State shall make or enforce any law which shall abridge the privileges or immunities of citizens of the United States; nor shall any State deprive any person of life, liberty, or property, without due process of law; nor deny to any person within its jurisdiction the equal protection of the laws.

Notes

www.ingramcontent.com/pod-product-compliance
Lightning Source LLC
Chambersburg PA
CBHW070703290526
45790CB00001B/433